Black Neighborhoods

Black Neighborhoods

An Assessment of Community Power

Donald I. Warren

Ann Arbor   The University of Michigan Press

Copyright © by The University of Michigan 1975
All rights reserved
ISBN 0-472-08960-9
Library of Congress Catalog Card No. 73-90888
Published in the United States of America by
The University of Michigan Press and simultaneously
in Don Mills, Canada, by Longman Canada Limited
Manufactured in the United States of America

To the late Frank A. Barcus, a proud citizen of Detroit

Contents

Introduction

SOCIAL SCIENCE has a schizoid character in American society. Why do I say this? Because often it is typified by obscurity of language and the limited utilization of its findings, yet at the same time, the popularization of theory and concepts drawn from behavioral science has frequently been singled out as the basis of ill-founded or misguided public policy.[1]

In the area of race and social research we have perhaps the epitome of the marginal status of social science. It is in this realm that the most vociferous and thorough-going attacks have been heaped upon this enterprise. Witness the words of Whitney Young—in his lifetime seen as a "moderate" versus a "militant" black leader:

My plan is for no more studies of Negroes this year. Think about it. Studying Negroes threatens to become one of the biggest businesses in the U.S. . . . . Every university has its 'Negro' expert, usually white. Every foundation is swamped with requests for funds to study this Negro ghetto or than one . . . don't get me wrong. I'm all for good scholarship. In fact Negro studying business has become so big that if we just end it quickly, too many people will be thrown out of work.[2]

Young's facetious commentary was presented in the same year (1968) that Martin Luther King, Jr. spoke, a few weeks before his death, to the Society for the Psychological Study of Social Issues. In his paper, "The Role of the Behavioral Scientists in the Civil Rights Movement," King indicated that "for social scientists, the opportunity to serve in a life-giving purpose is a humanist challenge of rare distinction."[3] He went on to say that "Negroes too are eager for a rendezvous with truth and discovery. We are aware that social scientists, unlike some of their colleagues in the physical sciences, have been spared the grim feelings of guilt that attended the invention of nuclear weapons. . . . Social scientists in the main are fortunate to be able to extirpate evil, not invent it."[4] At the same time King pointed out that "if the Negro needs social science for direction and for self-understanding, the white society is in even more urgent need. White America needs to understand that it is poisoned to its soul by racism and the understanding needs to be carefully documented."[5]

Sociology in particular has come under attack as a white institution which has perpetuated racism. Professor Stanley H. Smith at the 1972 Conference of Black Sociologists took the position that white sociologists cannot objectively examine "the black experience":

Sociologists who hold membership in the majority group tend to be concerned with adjustment to conditions as they exist in our present society. . . . The status quo oriented emphasis could conceivably be explained in terms of what seems to be a consistent predisposition on the part of the majority group sociologists to view the existence and life of minority groups . . . in terms of the pathological.[6]

Professor Wilson Record in the paper "White Sociologists and Black Studies" offers a further elaboration of the current relationship between the white sociologist and the black community:

The fundamentality of the challenge (of black activists) is exceeded only by its abruptness and feverish pace as a generator of crisis, which ended the brief golden hour of the white sociologists. They failed to predict the (black) move- ment, which now challenges their ability to predict anything. The golden hour began and ended in the 1960's. Supreme Court decisions and large-scale direct action by dissident blacks (and whites) had already moved race, and by impli- cation the white sociologist's specialty, to the center of the national stage. Then came the riots and . . . suddenly the white sociologists' expertise was in great demand not only by the liberal establishment . . . but even by the conservative corporations, unions, and school boards. . . .[7]

In Professor Record's survey of white sociologists who specialize in race he found that "a feeling of displacement . . . was painfully articulated by more than half of the 150 fellow sociologists I have interviewed."[8]

As Professor Record indicates, the charge of racism against liberal academics is a potent sting to conscience. The word coming out in 1968 and 1969 was certainly that any really nonracist researcher should be studying whites, not blacks.

With the growing estrangement between the sociological enterprise and the black community a presentation in the 1970s by a white researcher of a new research study in a major black community seems anachronistic at best and an exercise in institutional racism at worst.

My study carried out in Detroit during 1969 was not aimed at dramatic or topical analyses of riot or post riot issues. Instead the concern I have had as a student of urban life is focused on the persistence of ghettoization. In this context many persons—black and white —with whom I interacted in carrying out this type of research were skeptical and often uncomfortable.

I accept the mandate of Young and Dr. King that we have often, as majority-group social scientists, assumed that the position of blacks deviates from white norms. But the black ghetto and the black community have in many respects been ignored by American sociology—by its white as well as its black researchers.[9]

Yet I also made a major commitment early in the formulation of my research effort that, despite the flurry of ideological salvos, the black ghetto was an enduring fact of urban life. Riot studies in the main did not look at the social structural issues but instead focused on individual motivations, perceptions, and attitudes—of black youth and rioters as well as of white suburbanites.

The present study seeks mainly to test a set of major hypotheses about the distinctive nature of black population centers. In taking on this selective task I do not address a range of other urgent social policy and research issues. I do not intend to deal, for example, with whether the "real" power of changing black ghetto conditions does in fact largely rest in the hands of white institutions. Nor do I seek to explore the full ramifications of individual or institutional racism. Instead the major focus of my study is the uniqueness of the internal structure of black ghettoes vis-à-vis white centers of population.

In this pursuit of delimited research questions the basic design is comparative in character. Survey data from 932 black and 760 white respondents in the Detroit area provide the raw material for the study.[10] Essentially this approach represents a "snap shot" at one point in time and not the tracing of a set of processes over time. The creation and growth of the black urban ghetto is the background, given in terms of historic and demographic forces. What is tested in my research effort is the *perpetuation of black ghetto patterns*. In this sense I have sought to dip into the reality of ongoing processes. The parameters examined in my study are broad in scope and fundamental in character for any urban population.

I do not suggest that such a research effort captures the totality of black urban experience or even a part of it as seen by the persons immersed in its milieu. Instead I am interested in the explication of research findings which define the key sociological realities of black urban ghettoes. As such, the terminology and frame of reference are not geared to the "eyeball" level.

I do suggest that the life experiences of the black ghetto can be better understood by utilizing the concepts developed in this study. Moreover I believe that the perspective taken in this research permits the microcosmic and often fragmented view that the individual obtains of his own situation to be transformed and cumulated with the experiences of others. This in essence is my "bias." Sociological reality does not always correspond with individual perceptions. Social structural dynamics do not explain all of social reality.

To a large degree the exploration of my research findings and their implications are a provisional test of a set of evolving hypotheses. If data from several large metropolitan black ghettoes could be correlated, greater authority might be claimed for the conclusions I have reached. But all of this lies in the future. For the present the reader is invited to join the author on an intellectual excursion—not one that is merely an armchair set of speculations, but instead an interpretive approach to the complexities of urban social life in America's central cities. As such the end point is not merely academic precision in understanding but also a way to approach social action and planning.

Each chapter of this book will involve a central set of propositions and hypotheses relating to the distinctive character of the black urban ghetto. Our approach will be more narrative than monographic in character. We shall draw upon the empirical research from our Detroit data. In the main, however, statistical analysis and the presentation of tabular material will be illustrative, with more extensive findings contained in the Appendix tables.

Chapter I

Models of the Black Community:
Anchoring the Inquiry

What white Americans have never fully understood . . . is that white society is deeply implicated in the ghetto. White institutions created it, white institutions maintain it, and white society condones it.

> *Report of the National Advisory*
> *Commission on Civil Disorders*
> (Kerner Commission, 1968) p. vii

A NEW TERM has entered the vocabulary of America—"institutional racism." It is an important term, but one which is little understood. I shall forego the effort at a comprehensive definition. For it is precisely in the exploration of this neologism that one enters an unresolved dialogue about the nature of the black ghetto. By distinguishing institutional from other forms of racism (for example, personal bigotry and prejudice) we are immediately involved in such considerations as social class levels, power structure and organizational patterns. So we are speaking about social structure and the need to understand and assess these internal factors in order to grasp the essential nature of the black ghetto. Of course the simple recognition and acceptance into common parlance of the idea of institutional racism does not resolve the question of how and with what consequences black ghettoes relate to the dominant white society.

Let us approach the topic of the structural bases of racism by examining some of the most frequently evoked concepts of how the black and white communities are intertwined. We can identify three varieties of analysis or "models" which researchers, social commentators and community activists seem to employ. They are not necessarily independent of one another nor is it necessary to treat them as mutually exclusive. But each has a core focus—a special essence which serves as a springboard for both theorizing about change and shaping social policy and action. Once we have followed through these three approaches, we shall briefly introduce a fourth approach to be developed in our subsequent discussion.

The Isomorphism or Emulation Model

In his magnum opus on race, *An America Dilemma*, Gunnar Myrdal asserts that "Negro institutions are . . . similar to those of the white man. They show little similarity to African institutions. . . . Some peculiarities are even to be characterized as 'exaggerations' of American traits."[1] Discussing the voluntary associations of Blacks Myrdal states that "despite the fact that they are predominantly lower class, Negroes are more inclined to join associations than are whites; in this respect again, Negroes are 'exaggerated' Americans."[2] Myrdal goes on to say that:

Aside from the above-mentioned differences between Negro and white voluntary associations, they are much alike. Negro associations are apparently modelled after white associations, even if those white models are remnants of a past generation and so appear ludicrous to some white people today.[3]

This theory of emulation is caustically viewed by the eminent black sociologist E. Franklin Frazier:

The activities of "society" serve to differentiate the black bourgeoisie from the masses of poorer Negroes and at the same time compensate for the exclusion of the black bourgeoisie from the larger white community.[4]

Not all middle-class Negroes consciously desire . . . to be white in order to escape from their feelings of inferiority. . . . But when one studies the attitude of this class in regard to the physical traits or the social characteristics of Negroes, it becomes clear that the black bourgeoisie do not really wish to be identified with Negroes.[5]

Nathan Hare, a student of Frazier, in his book *Black Anglo-Saxons* provides a portrait of twelve varieties of white emulation and seeks to expose what he calls "the white norms they so blindly and eagerly ape." The gist of his thesis is that:

Black Anglo-Saxons are chiefly distinguishable in that, their struggle to throw off the smoldering blanket of social inferiority, they disown their own history and mores in order to assume those of the biological descendents of the white Anglo-Saxons. They relate to, and long to be part of, the elusive and hostile white world, whose norms are taken as models of behavior. White society is to most of them a looking-glass for taking stock of their personal conduct. . . . They must keep on grooming to make what they think white society imagines itself to be, accord with what they themselves would like to be: like whites.[6]

The Frazier-Hare polemic is usefully treated as a caricature rather than a description of but one segment of the black ghetto—the relatively affluent and highly educated. Even seen in that more limited frame, it might easily be dismissed as an anachronism: supplanted in the last few years by the more militant and nationalistic orientation of blacks in all income groups. If instead we take the "emulation" argument and translate it into *structural* terms—power, prestige, and organization—then it takes on a meaning that is less easily dismissed. Let us take for example the study which has become a classic in its own right, Floyd Hunter's *Community Power Structure*.[7] This sociologically oriented study of the decision-makers of Atlanta, Georgia, in the early 1950s introduced a powerful analytical tool as well as an ideological rallying cry. By "power structure" Hunter means the pyramid of leaders in a community who have the reputation for wielding influence and who know each other and provide a network of "influentials." Those at the very pinnacle—the "top" power circle —were mentioned as influentials by all or virtually all of Hunter's informants and they each named one another. (This "interlocking directorate" is closely akin to C. Wright Mills "power elite."[8])

Hunter found that in Atlanta the black community was excluded from the top levels of power. But he also discovered the blacks had a similar pyramid of power of their own. As he put it:

It may be said that the pattern of power leadership within the Negro community follows rather closely the pattern of the larger community. The method of turning up policy determining leadership was the same as used in the larger community. . . . From interviews with sub-community leaders the conclusion is clear that the process of decision on matters of policy rests with the top leaders as it does in the larger community.[9]

The key idea then is the "isomorphism" of black and white community power structures. Both systems have pyramidal forms of power even though one group is clearly subservient to the other in the total scheme of things. If this concept were to be depicted in graphic terms, we would have a white power structure represented as a larger hierarchy of top leaders and lesser influentials and next to it a miniature and duplicate of that arrangement for the black ghetto.

In the isomorphism model there can be some differences in the structure of the black ghetto which may be emphasized but do not detract from the structural similarities or identities of basic form with that of the white community. Andrew Billingsley in his analysis of black families reflects this point of view:

The various social forces described . . . have converged to form a pattern of social classes among Negro families not altogether unlike that in the general community, but with its own features reflecting the history and struggle for survival of the Negro people.[10]

The patterns of social stratification and social class in the black ghetto as described by St. Clair Drake are not completely identical in shape with the white community:

One of the most important effects of the income gap and the job ceiling has been the shaping of social class systems with Negro communities which differ markedly in their profiles from those of the surrounding white society. Negro class structure is "pyramidal," with a large lower class, a somewhat smaller middle class, and a tiny upper class. . . . White class profiles tend to be diamond shaped with small lower and upper classes and a larger middle class.[11]

The point is that while the basic class divisions which exist in the white community are also found in the black ghetto and the same standards are used to distinguish upper from lower class, the distribution of people in different strata is markedly different than in the white community.

Rejecting This First Model.   What are the drawbacks to using the "emulation" model of black ghetto social structure? First and perhaps most important is the denial of cultural distinctiveness. If we use the demographic indicators of income, occupation, and education patterns to evaluate community dynamics (even if they were to be identical for whites and blacks) quite different meanings or evaluations might result. As G. Franklin Edwards put it: "It is important to recognize that the Negro class structure and institutions have emerged in response to segregation and represent adjustments to the isolation under which Negroes have lived."[12] Several writers have stressed the interplay of demographic and cultural variables. Jessie Bernard suggests that "respectability" is the core of black ghetto class differences.[13] Billingsley states that "not only do absolute levels of education, income, and occupation take on somewhat different meanings in the Negro community, but factors other than these, including respectability and community activity loom large in the attribution of social status."[14]

There well might be a different meaning to the social stratification system (the way people are ranked and judged) in the black ghetto as compared to the surrounding white community. This fascinating hypothesis, implicitly or explicitly advanced by many writers is that the use of white standards of what constitutes higher or lower social status creates an illusion of false similarity between white and black populations. Census data and other "objective" measures may be false guides that fail to describe the "subjective" reality of black stratification.

In economic terms the black ghetto may be rife with poverty but the richness of social distinctions that arise escapes the measures of economic statistics. A good example of this is Elliot Liebow's *Tally's Corner*. In this study a group of men living on a single block in Washington D.C.'s ghetto reflect distinctive enough values and adjustments to life that their combination forms a kind of local neighborhood culture of its own.

There is a second major drawback to the emulation or isomorphism model of the black ghetto: it does not tell us about the dynamics of the black-white process of interrelations. In helping to explain or describe how power is exchanged between the two communities and what is the continuing effect of the white domination, the emulation approach is valueless. We do not know from this model how the white structure actually intervenes in the life of the black ghetto. If there is a top power leadership in the black ghetto that parallels that of the white power structure, are these the same kinds of people differing only in skin color? Is there really *any* true power in the black ghetto if it is like Hunter's Atlanta, a "subcommunity"?

The acceptance of the emulation model of the black ghetto or some variation of it forecloses any need to inquire about or describe the internal structure of the centers of urban black population. If it is merely a slightly skewed form of the white community, why bother to look further? One need only apply existing analyses of white class structure to the ghettoes, and to generalize about the black ghettoes on the basis of patterns found in white communities.

More dangerous is the invitation to government policy-makers and social agencies to use in black ghettoes strategies of change and community intervention that have proven effective in white communities. If poor white neighborhoods—especially Appalachian whites— have similar demographic patterns to poor blacks, the isomorphic model dictates that their problems be approached in the same manner. Thus both populations may be transient, come from the same region of the country, have high birth rates and low educational levels. But Appalachian whites in a Model Cities area may have few formal leaders and rely on very informal networks of relatives and friends for aid and social cohesion. Poor blacks may often live in neighborhoods where block clubs exist but they are largely for homeowners and not renters.

Or perhaps blacks on ADC (Aid for Dependent Children) are located in vast public housing tracts—islands of administratively created "neighborhoods"—isolated from the larger black or white areas beyond their own artificially "cohesive" and homogeneous subghetto.

Some blacks who are poor live cheek by jowl with middle income and even upper class groups. The riot areas of Detroit are a good example. The wealthy blacks of Boston and Chicago Boulevards live in formerly white-owned mansions and estate-like homes. They are school board officials and judges. A block or two away is Twelfth Street with its decay, rackets, vice, and dilapidated housing. That kind of heterogeneous neighborhood hardly ever exists in a white community. "Organizing" in that kind of neighborhood is a totally different matter from getting ADC mothers in a housing project to meet and work together and to participate in "their" community.

The two black settings I have described bear little resemblance, in community structure terms, to the poor white Appalachian areas, where any form of political organization involves bypassing the kin and neighbor ties that exist. On the other hand, blacks must use organizational forms like the block club when seeking contact with alien bureaucracies. The point is that concepts applicable in one cultural milieu can never be assumed to be transferable wholesale to another and are often empirically refuted by so doing.

The Ethnic Community Model

There is a common slogan nowadays when people talk about the problems of the black ghetto. It usually is stated in the following way: "Why can't they be like us?" In essence the questioner (presumed to be a member of a white ethnic group—Polish, Jewish, Italian, or one of many others) describes the struggles of his own people and wonders why there is great concern over the plight of blacks. The query is not necessarily a "racist" battle cry. It raises an important issue which needs careful analysis, namely: "How valid is the experience of the other ghettoized ethnic groups?"

Nathan Glazer, a leading figure in the sociological analysis of American urban life, makes a case for saying that blacks experience the same problems as white ethnic groups:

I believe it is possible to see the position of blacks in Northern cities in ethnic terms . . . to see them as the last of the major groups, the worst off, but due to rise over time to larger shares of wealth and power and influence.

... there is a great range in the experience of ethnic groups. They vary in time of arrival, skills at time of arrival, the character of the cities into which they come, the character of their cultural attributes, the degree of discrimination and prejudice they face. . . . In this range, the gap between the experience of the worst off of the ethnic groups and the Negroes is one of degree rather than kind.[15]

Glazer even suggests that blacks are better off than some white ethnic groups and have risen to higher positions in professional and community leadership roles.

Glazer is not saying that blacks have identical experiences to white ethnic groups but that when people make comparisons they must take into account the historical conditions at the time of movement to urban centers of a given group. Thus in terms of a national measure Glazer points out that blacks are more deprived as first comers to the United States but in terms of Northern cities they are late comers. Many eastern European immigrant groups were there first and their relatively better-off position reflects a longer assimilation period.

Glazer points out that analogies from one group to another can be deceptive. He suggests for instance that "the Irish showed remarkable political success, the Jews remarkable organizational and economic success, Japanese remarkable educational success, but Poles and Italians . . . were behind in all these areas." This range of experience according to Glazer, while it may put blacks near the bottom, it does not do so on a consistent or total basis.

In response to the white ethnic group analogy, Edwin Harwood, a co-author of *Life Styles in the Black Ghetto*, argues that the situation of contemporary American society is the major reason for rejecting this ethnic approach. The problem facing white immigrants was mainly one of cultural assimilation, not economics. He argues that "poverty did not have the same impact on European immigrants as it has had on rural American immigrants to the ghetto." In particular Harwood argues:

The foreign born had fewer of the basic amenities of life than today's slum dwellers—and certainly no systematic welfare services. Paradoxically, economic poverty has become a public issue among welfare professionals and social critics in part because things have been getting better. As our society has developed the resources to combat poverty with some hope of success, and as the growing affluence in other sectors of the society has made the poverty that still exists both more conspicuous and less acceptable, poverty has become a proper and realistic matter for attention.[16]

Harwood goes on to point out difficulties facing blacks which white ethnic groups did not have to contend with:

1. The renewal of transitional neighborhoods in the central cities has prevented some Negroes from acquiring housing of fairly good quality that they would have obtained in the normal course of events.

2. City-planning and good-government rhetoric has so dominated the public's view . . . that we tend to scoff at the idea that anything but harm could come from the earlier unplanned, spontaneous residential changes —what ecologists refer to as the "invasion and succession" of neighborhoods.

3. The ghettoized lower-class Negro has greater difficulty in getting to work. When the Europeans came to the city most of the industrial and commercial firms that could absorb them in large numbers were located near the city's core . . .

4. [On] the changed political culture . . . of the American city. . . . Whatever we may feel about the political machine and bossism, the machine did provide both avenues for mobility and resources for welfare which although inadequate from the standpoint of today's standards, were fairly well suited to the needs of the lower-class population.

5. "Personalizing" the law may have made the public peace easier to enforce. The evidence that has been accumulated from a number of sources indicates that the growing efficiency and impartiality of police and governmental agencies may actually lead to an increase of tensions in the ghettoes and an increasing feeling of alienation from city political authorities.[17]

Thus for Harwood, the conditions of black ghettoes reflect a scale of concentration and rapidity of inmigration which have no historic precedent in American society and which have occurred under special circumstances. The black ghetto is unique because it is so bureaucratized. It is unique because the "natural" population movements which occurred during earlier periods in American history are greatly accelerated and cannot provide for the evolution of adaptation mechanisms either by the external agencies of government or by the members of the ghettoized community themselves.

Harwood's argument is interesting precisely because he does not refute the essential historic facts described by Glazer. But he draws opposite conclusions from those of Glazer. Thus if blacks are late comers to urban centers Glazer says that we should use the position of white ethnic groups at earlier periods as a comparison, not their present position vis-à-vis blacks. Harwood seems to agree on the temporal sequence but says that structural conditions in the urban community—its institutions are now formalized and centralized— cannot be compared. Blacks can't rely on neighbors who are linked to city hall by family ties or associational "brotherhoods" as were the Irish. This same condition may also affect some of the remaining inner-city white ethnic groups such as Poles or Italians who are out of touch with power centers and decision-making structures of the metropolitan complex. Their more "assimilated" suburban peers may have escaped what Norbert Wiley calls "the ethnic mobility trap".[18]

The fact that communities like Hamtramck in the Detroit area or other "little Italys" have extensive forms of community life may mean simply that each has developed its own internal status and occupational hierarchy. Thus practicing law in an ethnic community, based on recognized educational and social status achievements, is a kind of pseudo-success. To practice law in a local ethnic community may cut one off from access to the corporate practice and larger power centers where the major decisions affecting local areas are actually made.[19]

So we have a kind of paradox about local ethnic enclaves based on territorial boundaries. In the contemporary structure of American society, being tied to the neighborhood or ghetto area is not a source of ethnic power but of ethnic powerlessness. Amitai Etzioni makes this point in arguing that "a group can maintain its cultural and social integration and identity without having an ecological base. . . . Ecological (spatial) ethnic groups are often less integrated into society than non-ecological. . . ."[20] In pursuing a case for "post-ghetto ethnic solidarity," he states:

The study of the natural history of Jews is focused around the concept of the ghetto. . . . It is a place and a state of mind, an area and an institution. This fusion is misleading at a decisive point, namely when the cultural group ceases to be confined to specific geographical boundaries. . . . The ecological approach reaches its limitations at the same point where the race-relations theory does not suffice. Neither concedes that members of the third (and later) generations of an ethnic minority may maintain a particular subculture, not lose their identity, although they are neither isolated nor concentrated in specific ecological (spatial) areas.[21]

Etzioni makes a case that ethnic groups pass through stages of change that may make physical proximity the poorest basis for community cohesion.[22] This developmental approach implies real differences of community form and not simply the absorption of the ethnic group into a broader community. Newly arrived immigrant groups may be viewed as at first interacting largely within a ghetto of physical dimensions and clear boundaries. During the second stage ghetto inhabitants begin to interact beyond these borders. The third stage involves the residential movement of people to some point beyond ghetto boundaries. During this same stage, however, many of the individuals who have "left" the ghetto still have friends and relatives living there. Neighborhoods have a "tipping point" so that a sufficient number of "block busters" is required to bring about this "boundary crossing" phase. In this same crucial third stage most formal social participation takes place largely within the confines of the ghetto.

During the final stage in this hypothetical sequence of change or evolution, immigrant groups both live and interact beyond the ghetto boundaries. Thus, residential dispersion in geographical terms under-estimates the solidarity of people who may maintain a nexus of social participation—formal and informal—within the same ethnic group, but who no longer live in close proximity to one another.

Problems of Applying the Ethnic Analogy to Blacks. We think there are several reasons for rejecting the application of the ethnic community model to the black ghetto. First of all, European immigrant groups have not encountered the extensive discrimination in housing that black Americans are so familiar with. Even those neighborhoods which are frequently labeled as "integrated" are often highly transitory in character. The adage that integration is "the time between the first black moving in and the last white moving out" is often applicable to a period of less than a decade in many urban centers of the United States.

Let us return to Etzioni's discussion of stages. The consequence for black Americans is that the sequential change process as we have conceptualized it for immigrant groups never passes beyond the third stage—that involving outside-the-ghetto residence and in-ghetto asso-ciational ties. As soon as upwardly mobile blacks move out of the ghetto they are confronted with the probability either of isolation from informal ties in a white neighborhood or the sudden change of that area with its influx of lower status blacks. Population is mobile but institutions remain the same. Or, more accurately, the cycle of reghettoization is maintained.

White ethnic groups are different from blacks not only in the likelihood that many become indistinguishable members of the anonymous majority community, but also that in *structural terms* territory no longer need be a basis of organization and power. Business and governmental organizations are no longer limited by being distant from customers and clients and gain cost economies by centralizing. The so-called organizational revolution reduces local efficiency and heightens the role of trained experts. For blacks the paradox of relatively sudden movement and apparent short-term advantages to geographical concentration may tend to perpetuate this first stage of "ghettoization" discussed by Etzioni. The growth is too rapid, the change in ghetto boundaries too tightly controlled by the majority power structure, and the internal variations in class and status among blacks too real to be neatly packaged.

For blacks the "ethnic mobility trap" often means that occupational structures such as welfare agencies and black entrepreneurial business are tailored to the "victim" roles of blacks. Blacks are forced to organize mainly around their victimization rather than upon a concept of gaining a major role in the larger institutional spheres of the community. This fact intensifies the uniqueness of the black ghetto as against white ethnic enclaves, since the relative affluence of some blacks becomes dependent on the persistence of the very character of the black ghetto's economic and social problems. Professionals in the black ghetto rise to positions of leadership in social service bureaucracies—church, welfare, drug-abuse programs, public schools, etc.—which are for the black ghetto consumption rather than production "industries." The by-product is that there is no change in the relationship between the ghettoized black community and the larger white society.

By contrast, many white ethnic groups gain power by their apparent "absorption" into the corporate structures of the majority, not mainly or even significantly by sponsored mobility into the highest circles of leadership, but simply through sharing the resources that are found in communities where such institutions are located, flourish, and must of necessity share their largesse.

The Colonial Analogy

We have rejected the notion of black ghettoes as autonomous miniatures of white communities, and we also cannot accept the view of simply comparing blacks to a white ethnic group. In recent years there has been advanced and widely discussed the proposition that the ghetto is similar to an overseas dependency. As this perspective has gained prominence it has challenged more traditional approaches and stimulated much polemical debate but little empirical research. One of the most closely argued analyses using the colonial model is that presented by Robert Blauner. The essential argument of his position is contained in the following passages from the article entitled "Internal Colonialism and Ghetto Revolt":

Of course many ethnic groups in America have lived in ghettoes. What makes the black ghettoes an expression of colonized status are three special features. First, the ethnic ghettoes arose more from voluntary choice, both in the sense of choice to immigrate to America and the decision to live among one's fellow ethnics. Second, the immigrant ghettoes tended to be a one and two generation phenomenon; they were actually waystations in the process of acculturation and assimilation. . . . The black ghetto on the other hand has been a more permanent phenomenon, although some individuals do escape it.

But most relevant is the third point. European ethnic groups . . . only experienced a brief period, often less than a generation, during which their residential buildings, commercial stores, and other enterprises were owned by outsiders. . . . But Afro-Americans are distinct in the extent to which their segregated communities have remained controlled economically, politically, and administratively from the outside.[23]

The colonial analogy of Blauner and others stresses the economic class aspects of racism. William Tabb, another exponent of the colonial thesis, states that the "marginal working class" which makes up so much a part of the black ghetto permits the capitalist class "to isolate segments of the working class from each other" and to strengthen its control "by creating a marginal working class of blacks and giving white workers a relatively more privileged position."[24] In pointing out that the economic relations of the black ghetto to white America "closely parallel those between third world nations and the industrially advanced countries," Tabb points to the demographic basis of the colonial analogy:

The ghetto . . . has a relatively low per capita income and high birth rate. Its residents are for the most part unskilled. Businesses lack capital and managerial know-how. Local markets are limited. The incidence of credit default is high. Little saving takes place in the ghetto, and what is saved is usually not invested locally. Goods and services tend to be "imported" for the most part, only the simplest and the most labor-intensive are produced locally. The ghetto is dependent on one basic export—its unskilled labor power. Aggregate demand for the export does not increase to match the growth of the ghetto labor force and unemployment is prevalent. Cultural imperialism is also part of the relationship; ghetto schools traditionally teach the history of the 'Mother Country' as if blacks had no identity of their own, no culture, no origins worthy of mention. . . . The dominant culture is constantly held up as good, desirable, worthy of emulation. The destruction of the indigenous culture is an important weapon in creating dependence and reinforcing control.[25]

In making his case Tabb and the other advocates of the colonial analogy focus their attention on the *interaction*—the exchange across the ghetto boundaries. This is an important concept because the notion of the black ghetto as an isolated "subcommunity" or "subsystem" is a factor which the ethnic group approach and isomorphism models tend to ignore. They do this because they view structure in static terms. While it is valuable to say how the ghetto was formed and what "shape" it has, the colonial model stresses *process*—the dynamics of community institutions as an interdependent system.

Limitations of the Colonial Model. The colonial model, even as Tabb elaborates it, presumes a high level of economic stagnation and this in turn implies an *absolute* rather than a *relative* deprivation vis-à-vis whites. A number of the studies of rioters in Detroit, Los Angeles, and Newark indicate that the most active groups were not those at the bottom of the economic ladder, but those feeling "relatively" deprived. If indeed the marginal working class of the black ghetto are the major victims of racism and economic exploitation, it is clear that others in the ghetto have more resources, education, and the values to press for change and the return of ghetto control to its inhabitants.

Consequently, the colonial analogy ignores some of the internal ghetto dynamics that may or may not be simply the manipulation of the outside ruling structure. Thus Tabb speaks of a growing bifurcation within the black community:

> The middle class blacks assuming positions in the wider society will be increasingly called upon to keep the lid on things by whites and at the same time will be under pressure from below to identify with the continuing black struggle. . . .
> The colonial analogy becomes misleading when it is used to suggest the possibility of meaningful black independence within the context of American Society. As the size of the black middle class increases, the cohesiveness of common racial identity may be lessened and a long term sustained effort to achieve independence made even more difficult. At the same time strengthening the black community's economic and political power increases its bargaining position vis-à-vis the white society.[26]

In effect Tabb is saying that the gains of middle class blacks pose as much of a threat to black solidarity as the intervention of the white colonial structure. On one level it might be argued of course that this "co-optation" strategy is quite deliberate and is just a more sophisticated control device by white society.

Regardless of the motivation or white machinations ascribed to the increased social mobility experienced by some blacks, its implications for internal black ghetto structure clearly involve greater diversity of status and greater distance from the top to the bottom of the social order in the black ghetto. As a result the very diversity of the black ghetto, rather than its monolithic "lumpenproletariat" character, serves as an important description of reality—what the black ghetto is actually like. In purely Marxist terms, the class structure of the

black ghetto becomes a fulcrum of social conflict and social order. As
these dynamics emerge in the black ghetto the role of the local black
middle income group (capitalists and others) may become more salient
than the less visible but still significant white institutional structures.
All of which makes the colonial model increasingly abstract as a basis
for understanding the growth and differentiation of the black ghetto.

The ironic tendency among most proponents of the colonial
analogy is to see "cultural imperialism" as identical with economic
imperialism; students of colonialism in the international sphere have
found it useful to separate these varieties and indicate which is
paramount in a given situation.

If the ghetto is a colony in cultural terms, then the task of social
change is not simply one of ridding the populace of "outside" control,
but of reconstructing the entire base of black life in cities. Many
adherents of revolutionary change, economic and cultural, find this
obvious and perfectly logical. For others interested in major social
change, this leaves no set of intermediary steps or useful avenues for
ending racism in the short run. Like some of the abstract goals of
traditional Marxism, the vision of taking over the former white
colonies, in this case the American black urban ghettoes, seems to
involve a combination of precisely timed overthrow of the oppressor
with interspersed periods of passive observation of historic events such
as resistence to being co-opted, avoiding irrelevant "token" actions,
etc. Since the structure is destined to rot by its own nature, only
revolutionary action is meaningful.

An Alternative Approach: The "Social Compression" Concept

None of the approaches we have outlined is lacking in valuable insights.
Yet they all have two faults in common: they are not rooted in a body
of systematic empirical data and they ignore the need to connect present
day realities with social policy. As intriguing abstractions they may
suffice to gratify the ideological needs of some black activists and
white liberals and intellectuals. All presume that either we have the
knowledge to act but power-holders resist or that the very development
of history makes any particular action or further inquiry irrelevant
and diversional.

Particularly since the end of white paternalism and control is
seen as the first and most urgent step in the achievement of black
psychological well-being and economic justice, it is difficult to argue

that policy-makers and activists in the black community should be concerned with what is left to be done once "power is transferred." But it is precisely because the black ghetto is a social fact in both an historical and sociological sense that it will continue to shape future social realities and therefore ought to be focused on as a phenomenon sui generis. This perspective rests on two major points:

1. The fact that a highly differentiated community cannot seek growth and development by a stress on unity alone. Monolithic solutions to black ghetto problems have not proven effective even when major economic investments have been made from the outside.

2. From a sociological point of view black urban ghettoes are structurally complex and in many ways more diverse than similarly sized white populations.

With these two points in mind we shall seek an empirically based model for the internal structure of black ghettoes which takes account of those processes and historic factors that have shaped the present character of such communities.

The black ghetto must be viewed as generative of specific institutional patterns that set it apart as a structural reality. Central to that character is the role of neighborhood heterogeneity, social class diversity, spatial compression, and the interrelations of these factors with one another. Those are the tools of our analysis. Economic factors alone, formal political structure alone, family life alone, cultural values alone do not exhaust the meaning of what the black ghetto is. Instead we shall use the data gathered from sixteen black and twelve white neighborhoods in the Detroit area and we shall summarize, extrapolate, and generalize about local neighborhoods and organizational networks in order to examine the state of black communities in terms of these critical middle levels of social power.

Chapter II

The Black Ghetto as a Spatial System

In the vocabulary of the social scientist and the social worker there must be few words used with either the frequency or looseness as "community." It is one of those terms which as Le Bon said, are uttered with solemnity, and as soon as they are pronounced an expression of respect is visible on every countenance, and all heads are bowed.

N. Dennis, "The Popularity of the
Neighborhood Community Idea," in
R. E. Dahl (ed.), *Readings in Urban Sociology*
(Pergamon Press, 1968), p. 74

"THEY'RE BURNING DOWN THEIR OWN COMMUNITY!" So runs a paraphrase of a common white response to the events of August 1965 in the Watts area of Los Angeles. Again we hear the refrain in the aftermath of the hot week in July 1967, when the Twelfth Street area of Detroit erupted. The Hough area of Cleveland as a symbol of black anger also springs to mind. Then Milwaukee, Indianapolis, and Washington, D.C., following the assassination in May 1968 of Dr. Martin Luther King, Jr. Strangely, one location is absent from the list: a teeming concentration of black families in New York City: Bedford-Stuyvesant.[1]

The litany of black ghettoes which emerged into national prominence in the last decade conveys a content of violence, fear, repression, and for many black and white persons sensitive to the human condition, a bewilderment and awakening of new despair about urban life. When the debris is cleared from the streets, and the burned-out homesteads and businesses are demolished, some fundamental questions persist: why then? why in that place? why did the black ghetto explode?

The myths are plentiful, several explanations seem plausible: social protest, alienation, the discontent of the poverty stricken.[2] But then some unanswered queries and incongruous facts remain. In Detroit, for example, the neighborhoods where rioting was most prevalent were not the worst slum areas of the black or white community. Yet the Model Cities Program in Detroit (just beginning at the time of the 1967 "hot summer" but clearly defined by local administrators) barely touched the major sites of burning and looting in that summer of agony.[3] Second, individuals who have been interviewed and jailed do not fit the stereotyped picture of "riff-raff" or teenage rebels. Yet another fact is that burning and looting was selective and had support in some neighborhoods, opposition in other areas. There was a pattern, not elaborated or planned, but clear evidence of shared goals and structure in much of what happened.[4]

Few observers of Detroit's second major racial disturbance of the last thirty years would deny its significance for the black community as well as the white. A very strong case can be made that the events of that July week in 1967 brought pride and a sense of cohesion to blacks, and shocked whites into awareness of the power of blacks in Detroit.

How is it possible to consider the sudden, sporadic, and seemingly "irrational" behavior of "rioters" in Detroit to form an important measure of black solidarity? Surely this is a somewhat ludicrous and unfair comparison. But it brings into focus even more basic questions: Is there a relationship between the proximity of blacks as a population and the emergence of a black community? What is the relationship between the term "community" and the concept of "ghettoization"? This latter term often is a connotative one, calling forth ideas such as poverty, overcrowding, social pathology, and other negative images. The psychological burden of living in such an area includes the notion of "ghetto mentality"—a parochialism of mind and restricted sense of self-worth. Equally subjective is the meaning we tend to ascribe to the word "community." The "sense of common values," "consciousness of kind," "cohesion" and adherence to "shared norms" denote the kinds of positive images associated with community.

Can we gain any answer to the query raised at the beginning of our discussion as posed by the puzzled white onlooker of black neighborhood "civil disorders"? Perhaps we need to ask further what the black community is or, more exactly, what is the *nature* of the black community. Let us sharpen the issue even more: what is the nature of the black community in urban black ghettoes?

Such an inquiry guided the project on black and white neighborhoods which the author carried out in the Detroit area in 1969 and 1970. The impetus for this research sprang from a conviction that the black areas of urban cities are not merely economically deprived and culturally distinct areas, but that they have fundamentally unique *structural* forms. We started with a hypothesis that the black ghetto has a location in space and that this fact is the result of distinct social forces. *These social dynamics lead us also to argue that the black ghetto is perhaps not a community at all.*

The Black Ghetto as an Ecological Unit

Human ecology as a distinctive branch of modern sociology deals with the interdependence of a population. Most often it takes as indicators of the basic system of life in a community the spatial patterns that it manifests.[5] From the standpoint of human ecology, attitudes and values are imbedded in the neighborhood, land use, and economic specialisms that are found in different areas of a city or town.

If there is a cultural distinctiveness attached to a given physical locale, it is derived from and expressed in the observable delineations of types of housing, clustering of businesses, and outward appearance of local institutions. Most central of all in the human ecology equation is the premise that *forms* of adaptation to the total environment of a population are a property of that group as a whole and are not to be confused with subjective states of mind or mere "psychological" facts.[6] In other words individuals may compose a given population but the processes of coping and survival need a set of institutionalized responses which express themselves in geographical terms.

Is it meaningful then in human ecological terms to speak about the distinctiveness of the "black ghetto"? The answer in our view is categorically *yes*. The black ghetto is a phenomenon "sui generis."[7] The rich tradition of the so-called Chicago School of sociology, which flourished beginning in the 1920s, gave rise to one of the classical pieces of literature on black communities, Drake and Cayton's *Black Metropolis*. In their introduction, the authors tell us: "Walk the streets of the Black Belt and you will find . . . beneath the surface are patterns of life and thought attitudes and customs, which make Black Metropolis a unique and distinctive city within a city. Understand Chicago's Black Belt and you will understand the Black Belts of a dozen large American cities."[8] Ghettoization as a dynamic process therefore refers not simply to a fixed place but to a fixed structure as well. It is the replication of a set of social organizational patterns. These forms—the morphology of the ghetto—are critically defined by the local neighborhoods in which black urban populations reside.[9]

Such dynamics are not attributable to the state of mind of individuals, although those are real enough; not simply to a set of economic relationships, although those are extremely significant; nor merely to a set of power relationships as seen from the standpoint of whites and blacks. Instead, we argue that all of these processes we see operating "above the water line" do not themselves reveal the "true" nature of black urban ghettoes. Once we recognize the formative elements of such communities, we must inevitably come to the view that economic change alone, the alteration of power positions within the community, and remolding ideological perspectives and attitudes of the young are all alterations that would not attack nor obliterate the social forces of territorial organization of the urban black ghetto.

Using the tools of human ecology we are able to identify a set of social forces often masked by the strivings and agonies and surface conflicts between individuals. Taken in the light of a focus on the structure of ecological forces, such events are largely "epiphenomena" —mere by-products of the more basic forces shaping black urban life.

What are these forces? We can place these within the following dynamic processes:

1. Structural growth—the incorporation of varying forms of local neighborhoods, often including rapid "succession" or "invasion" vis-à-vis previous populations

2. Differentiation-stratification—increasingly diverse life styles and socioeconomic levels confined in relative "compression," given restricted growth of the boundaries of the unit

3. Formalization-Institutionalization—the development of inherited and continuing patterns of informal and formal organizational styles and structures

4. Isolation with lack of closure—the monopolization of geographical areas due to the ending of competition by other groups for land within the "ghetto," coupled with lack of independence from the larger community in shaping the internal dynamics of the "subordinate" population

If we examine each of these processes we find principles that apply in all social and biological systems. The term "ecology" refers to the interrelations of differing elements composing a system of life. Even in the case of human organizations, such as corporations, schools, and voluntary associations, increases in size are accompanied by the need for established rules, set lines of authority, and the minute categorization of individuals. The tasks of such social units are coordinated by established norms, not by improvised solutions.

So it is in the ghetto. At first, the uprooted migrant arrives as the better educated, upwardly bound move on. But over time, youth grows up in the ghetto not with newly developed attitudes, but with established norms and rules that fit the needs of the ghetto. Leadership, which is at first diffuse or nonexistent, becomes formalized and stratified. In the same way, failure becomes clearly defined at several levels of the ghetto. A by-product of growth is the definition of elaborate status positions, levels of achievement, styles of life, and political power. All of these become increasingly sharp in their outline. Just as the mature bureaucratic organization has set rewards and status positions, so does the ghetto community. In the same way in which a manufacturer increases efficiency by subdividing work and standardizing the components of production, so the ghetto sifts and sorts its members by skill—legitimate and illegitimate. Age groups, occupational groups, religious groups, and other special elements of the community emerge as increasingly disparate and specialized entities. The product of their combined efforts is never immediately at hand, but always remains in the abstract, whether this be ad hoc protest, orderly demonstrations, or simply the task of adjusting to the outer white community.

Finally, the interweaving of growth processes results in a distinct phenomenon—a tangible unit with dimensions at once physical, social, and psychological. Increasingly, the ghetto life is self-enforcing. It produces an ever sharper basis for defining one's position in life—a separate one from the amorphous, often disturbing world of the non-ghetto limbo.

Each of these ideas we have exemplified refers to a basic social process which is at the same time internal to the black ghetto and a result of the interaction between the black population and the larger white majority community. This is a key idea in our approach and it is this "exchange" or "interaction" process which distinguishes our analysis from one in which black communities are independent and self-regulating expressions of distinctive societies. Essential to our view is that determinism and uniqueness coexist and must both be utilized in understanding the reality of black urban ghettoes.

Principles of Growth and the Black Ghetto

The analysis of human communities and that of plant and animal ecology have had a history of mutual borrowing. When we speak about "adaptation" of a human population and the principles governing change in human society, we are able to understand these in part from the use of biological analogies. Let us take a set of growth principles. Are there "laws" of human communities that can be applied? Mason Haire, in examining the growth of large organizational structures, has pointed out the concept of the "cube to square equation."[10] By this formula Haire points out that as a structure increases in size, sensitivity and contact with the larger environment increase even faster. He illustrates this principle by analogy to what happens if the diameter of a sphere is doubled with the result that the surface of the sphere—its contact area—increases threefold. If we transfer this growth principle to a population with a given structure, then the expansion of that group would imply far greater points of contact with the external world than the increases in interaction among its own members. Put in a somewhat different way, if a community seeks to utilize the resources of the total environment in which it is located, restriction to a two-dimensional areal location limits access to resources. Let us focus this particularly in the light of organizational networks.

In a study conducted at the time of the Detroit riot, a team of researchers[11] plotted the location of voluntary association memberships of a sample of blacks and whites in the Detroit SMSA (Standard Metropolitan Statistical Area). Using a methodology based on the construction of an ellipse of spatial meeting points for social interaction, the researchers found that the mean ellipse for whites was 48 square miles and for blacks 13 square miles. Each person interviewed had indicated on a map where he went for meetings of the groups to which he belonged. The conclusion reached by the research group was that black associational patterns were greatly restricted in the urban space of the Detroit metropolitan community (see figure 1).

Kenneth Boulding, in discussing principles of social change and related biological growth models, refers to the idea of "nonproportional growth."[12] In essence this law of growth states that all biological organisms must change their form or structure as they surpass a particular size limit. This principle makes all of the science fiction plots concerning gargantuan insects represent a biological impossibility. Without developing entirely new structural elements, such as a skeletal system, organisms of small size cannot grow beyond fixed limits. Growth in both social and biological systems is inextricably linked with structural change.

What is the implication of the law of nonproportional change for

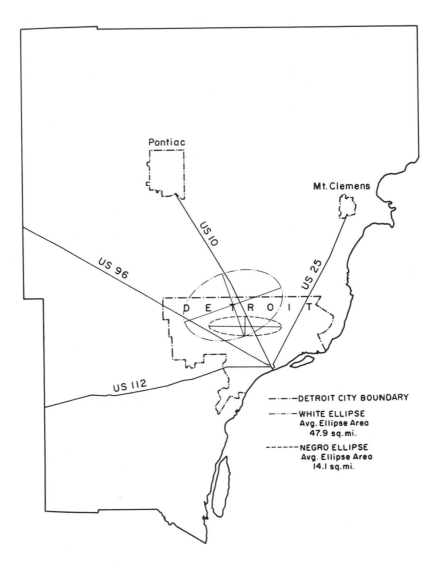

Fig. 1. Interaction Ellipses, Detroit Standard Metropolitan Statistical Area, 1965. (From R. V. Smith, S. E. Flory, and R. L. Bashshur, *Community Interaction and Racial Integration in the Detroit Area: An Ecological Analysis,* Eastern Michigan University, project no. 2557, U.S. Office of Education, September 8, 1967.)

black ghettoes? If we note that during the 1960s black populations grew by 20 percent, while for whites the gain was only 12 percent, and that continued in-migration to black urban areas was at a high level, then we have conditions which suggest strong needs for institutional change in black centers of population. New forms of organization along with the need to join together such expressions of community linkage are required. Mere replication of the same types of organizations used by other populations does not respond to the requirements of the structural modifications implied by the principle of nonproportional growth. A good case in point is the role of block clubs in predominantly black neighborhoods. Such groups can serve as important expressions of "grass roots" problems, but must in turn be linked to other organizations in order to make an impact on the major power centers of the community. Federations of such clubs have sprung up in Detroit and other black population centers. Yet the resulting decision-making hierarchy and the sheer need to communicate "up the ladder of organization" often negates the value of a territorial system of community involvement of this type. If formal bureaucracies have difficulty in responding quickly and effectively to new problems and concerns, then the construction of elaborate layers of local community participation often\result in similar if not even poorer response to people's basic needs and concerns.

Our argument in regard to the black ghetto is that its use of the more informal, intimate, face-to-face or what sociologists call "primary group" structures to respond to community needs under conditions of relatively small population size no longer are appropriate to the current needs of black urban dwellers. If black ghettoes merely proliferate the same organizational forms under conditions of growth and diversification of population, the effectiveness of such institutions will be increasingly limited.

Retention of outmoded institutional solutions to current problems in black ghettoes results, in some measure, from the pseudo-cohesion suggested by territorial primacy and black population concentration. But, to use a phrase from a satirical skit popular some years ago, "there can be proximity without relating." Ghettoization results in undue reliance on territorial bases, structures, and organizations which are appropriate to a more intimate form of small community life.

Population compression imposes an emphasis on territorial organization which is, in the contemporary society of cosmopolitan corporate styles, a basis for sustaining powerless institutions. One example of this is the interest expressed by many white liberals and some black organizations in "black capitalism." Often it takes the form of advocating more local black businesses and the transfer of ownership from the traditional, marginal, and often despised white ethnic entrepreneur to the new black ghetto small businessman. These programs of change in the ghetto ignore the structural realities of contemporary American society. Locally oriented black capitalism is the economic equivalent of using block clubs to change major conditions of housing and city services whose institutional levers lie elsewhere.

In assessing the nature of population growth and the character of ghetto responses we can begin to see that the query "why are they burning their own neighborhoods?" is based on a false analogy between white and black community settings. This question really implies a model appropriate to the New England village where a community was built up from the local institutions through a natural system of ties to the top power centers.[13] For blacks to accept such a model requires the view that local ghetto neighborhoods are foundations of a power base when, in fact, they may be distractions from the "real" sources of community control.

Differentiation-Stratification. The emergence of large concentrations of black residents in central cities under conditions of restricted areal growth has implications for social class. Studies in social stratification from the time of the Lynds' classic *Middletown*[14] and the work of W. Lloyd Warner[15] and his associates, have emphasized the intimate link between class and territoriality. Dispersion of individuals with given occupational, educational, and life-style orientations toward association with like-minded persons represents a natural process in the growth of human populations.

But this process in black urban ghettoes has been altered. Taueber and Taeuber in their major demographic work, *Negroes in Cities*, note that:

Judging from fragmentary sources, it appears that the amount of class segregation in the Negro community is, on the whole, less than that found among white populations. Similar analyses for whites in Cleveland and Chicago indicate not only a greater amount of occupational differentiation for whites in these cities, but also little change in the level of differentiation between 1950 and 1960. The lesser average degree of class segregation among Negroes is probably due not only to the limitations on the housing supply imposed by racial residential segregation, but also to the less degree of occupational diversity among the Negro population.[16]

While growth in numbers need not imply that a population becomes more diversified in its characteristics, the forces which have shaped black urban ghettoes have also tended to increase differentiation among members of the black community. Such a process has been commented upon by many persons involved in the changes of the past several decades in such cities as Chicago, New York, and Detroit. This increased diversity of the black community stems from two factors: demographic forces outside the black community itself, and the interaction between patterns of regional migration and separateness of ghetto life accompanying increases in population.

Thus one can discern in the history of black urban communities in the twentieth century a pattern in which relatively small and highly developed black communities existed as entities comparable to the more recent influx of European white ethnic groups. With the employment booms of World Wars I and II, these original black communities expanded with the accompanying upward mobility of many of the white ethnic groups. Blacks moved into formerly white neighborhoods because of the pressure of population from internal expansion. But this expansion was expressed mainly at those points in the surrounding community which were most permeable and represented the "vulnerable" locations along the imposed boundary line of the white community. Consequently the degree of job mobility and educational change in the larger black community has not been matched by a similar expression of territorial differentiation.[17]

Our basic thesis about black ghetto social structure is that physical compression cannot restrict social diversification. The population of black ghettoes not only grows in size but becomes more varied in social class and status terms. Therefore, in contrast to the white majority, blacks live in local neighborhoods that often reflect less homogeneity of class, values, or life style than do many suburbs and small urban centers. Expansion for the black ghetto therefore becomes synonymous with heterogeneity derived from the fixed or relatively fixed community boundary. For a neighborhood to attain a black majority is sufficient to have it declared part of the ghetto—the very definition emanating from the exodus of white residents. Thus even the most affluent blacks cannot alter this process of demarcating the ghetto's limits.

The greater occupational similarity of all-white compared to all-black neighborhoods in Cleveland and Chicago is fully elaborated by Eugene Uyeki.[18] The subjective meaning of this status heterogeneity is alluded in Powdermaker's study of the South:

Side by side live the respectable and the disrespectable, the moderately well-to-do and the very poor, the pious and the unsaved, the college graduates and the illiterates, the dusky blacks, the medium browns, the light creams, all thrown together because all are Negroes.[19]

Andrew Billingsley suggests the complexity of black stratification:

Not only do absolute levels of education, income, and occupation take on somewhat different meanings in the Negro community, but factors other than these, including respectability and community activity loom large in the attribution of social status.[20]

In writing a new introduction to *The Negro Ghetto*, Robert Weaver saw class conflict looming as a larger factor than ever in black ghettoes:

In 1947 the ghetto was oppressive to Negroes of all economic and social classes. Today some Negroes of higher income are able to escape from residentially segregated areas. . . . In the interim the exodus of some middle-class nonwhites from areas of minority group concentration has contributed another problem. It is the class dichotomy between the masses of low-income and destitute nonwhites and the more affluent. As a consequence, class, as well as race, has become significant in the Negro community.[21]

The fact of greater social class differentiation within the black ghetto may be seen to be more than a quantitive difference vis-à-vis white populations. Thus, Jay Williams, in studying the bases of social stratification which were highly predictive for whites, found that, when applied to a black population, these bases do not correlate as significantly. He suggests, in fact, that the bases of stratification may differ for the black community compared to the white community.[22]

Not only the amount of interstratum contact is increased in the black ghetto compared to other communities, but the very nature of social status takes on different meanings. Kenneth Clark provides a most eloquent description of such a dynamic:

A member of the Negro middle class may both idealize and reject the masses of working class Negroes. A working class Negro may at the same time be proud of the skill and poise of Negro leaders and resent and suspect them because of their education and achievement. . . . The present unrealities and distortions of ghetto life make it difficult to differentiate between empty flamboyance and valid achievement; . . . those who have been deeply damaged by the ghetto seem unable to trust their own feelings. They cannot afford the psychic luxury of depth of emotion. . . . The same person might move from indifference to adoration to condemnation of a fellow Negro within a single conversation without his or her audience's seeming to be conscious of any inconsistency.[23]

The key thesis that must be advanced at this point is that "ghetto" means complexity of group structure. It refers to a series of cultures (subcultures) existing side-by-side. Ghetto, if it has any significance as an abstraction refers to a pattern of compression, the compacting of many status groups in a restricted physical environment. If we begin exploring the ghetto by using the tools we have indicated, we are led to examine the range of individual perceptions, attitudes, beliefs, behaviors, of a variety of ghetto inhabitants.

Formally Perpetuating the Black Ghetto. In the terminology of social science, "institutionalization" is the process by which given patterns of behavior found useful at one point in time by a group are developed into ongoing and inherited patterns imposed on each new generation of group members. "Formalization" is that aspect of the institutionalization process in which definable roles and organizational forms emerge to carry forth the traditional behavior patterns. The storefront church, the block club, visible and intense "street life"—these are some of the patterns which persist even in suburban black neighborhoods.

As expressions of the institutional complex of a population, such forms provide important ways to say that the "ghettoization" process to which black urban dwellers are exposed is to be sharply differentiated from the experience of white ethnic groups. It is important to confront the commonly held view that blacks are just a slightly more visible ethnic group. Our analysis of ghetto social structure disputes this analogy. Our rejection of the comparison to white ethnic ghettoes rests on two issues: the rate of assimilation of former ghetto ethnic groups into the larger society, and the retention of previous formal and informal cultural patterns by European and other nonblack migrants to urban areas. We are saying that one unique aspect of the rigidity of black ghetto organizations and local institutions is the lack of interplay between a former cultural milieu, a new environment, and contact between assimilated and nonassimilated members of the group. Many of the European ethnic groups have experienced diffusion of their members throughout a large population center within the span of one or two generations. The result is that the temporary adjustment to a highly compacted ghetto life of the new immigrant has not become a tradition handed down as a cultural heritage. Where white ethnic groups were required to discard many cultural patterns in their absorption into American urban centers, the most formal institutions —church and voluntary association organizations—were retained, albeit in modified form in many instances. At the same time the more primary-group and intimate structures were protected by the very process of population concentration. For white ethnic groups the most difficult "adjustment" to American urban society has been the linkage between values of family and neighborhood and church versus the demands of formal education, occupational mobility, and geographic mobility.

Historically, both the Jews and Italians had organizational structure prior to their location in ghettoes in this country. They began to lose their group identity, common geographic locale, and the total network of linking institutions once affluence was widely shared in the community. While this tended to flow from the affluence of the surrounding society, it is nevertheless true that organization preceded ghettoization, affluence followed organization, and finally deghettoization followed affluence. These processes are not historically comparable to black communities where organization has followed ghettoization, and affluence has preceded, to a large degree, effective "ethnic" organization.

Why has the situation for blacks been so different? First of all, many of the institutional forms which have formal characteristics in the black ghetto—church, voluntary association, and neighborhood groups— are not really cultural inheritances from a historical social structure but inventions of the urban ghetto itself. Moreover, those patterns of associations which are primary-group in character have been divorced from mobility, economic, occupational, or educational institutions and goals. Blacks have not been faced with the choice of clinging to local neighborhood and family patterns versus moving into larger structures of the society to the same degree as have white ethnic groups. In the case of the New Deal and such civil service hierarchies as the U.S. Postal Service, some informal links of family and bureaucracy occurred. Friends, neighbors, and relatives might well be in the same work organization. But these have been rare exceptions. Blacks have not had the choice of localized "ethnic" occupations versus entering the more cosmopolitan and "impersonal" corporate world even at the price of losing some ethnic identity.

Since many enclaves of white ethnic groups represent only fractional portions of the individuals who trace their roots to a specific ethnic area or background, those parts of urban centers which have remained as white ethnic localities are still not comparable to black urban ghettoes. These residual areas of immigrant concentration may be romanticized and, as in the case an area like Hamtramck, Michigan, represent a major center of continuing ethnic domination in population terms. But the inhabitants of such segments of the urban area are influenced largely by a *selection* rather than a socialization process.

They are either older residents with particular occupational or family patterns who for economic or value commitment reasons stay put. By contrast, few members of such communities remain because of the strong molding of their values implied by what sociologists term "attitudinal socialization." This latter process of continuing influence and social reinforcement is more likely to take place where a group has little control over who comes into the community while there is little opportunity for exit from it.

The Ghetto as an Isolated but Not Closed Social System.   To the extent that black populations become highly compressed and segregated in urban space a clear "boundary" emerges. This is not a fixed frontier but represents a point of exchange. The economy within the ghetto involves services which are unique in terms of locational concentration. Louis Ferman has termed these occupations as an "irregular economy" involving "jack-of-all-trades" and "odd-job" roles.[24] In addition, organized prostitution and narcotic and gambling distribution systems centralize in the ghetto but are utilized by nonghetto persons or eventually reach such persons outside of its boundaries. Exchange at the ghetto boundary also means that some former residents of an area return for friendship and organizational participation reasons while others living in mainly black neighborhoods travel far from the local setting to be active in groups outside of the ghetto.

There is a clearly important subjective and perceptual or attitudinal boundary to the black ghetto. This was exemplified in a major incident of racial confrontation following the shootout known in Detroit as the "New Bethel incident."[25] Survey findings indicated that white persons accepted the interpretation of the media as to what happened—black militants had ambushed two white police officers. The ghetto had no way to protect its interests in terms of the intensification of white fear and hostility. Among blacks interviewed who had relied on the white TV or newspaper media, there was a general tendency to suspend judgment as to whether the blacks involved were at fault or the police. In this situation the mass media could not be used by blacks as sources of information about the larger community and in particular about an incident involving whites and blacks. Were the black press to have reporters and resources to obtain the news about what occurs at the boundary and beyond the black ghetto itself, symmetrical institutional links could reduce racial polarization. Instead, the ghetto is isolated from the external spheres of policy-making and is, at the same time, forced to resist access by external institutions which tend to be either directly or indirectly exploitive. Thus, either as a protective measure or because of the established history of not being able to screen any of the outside influences coming into the community, ghetto institutions move toward autonomy from those outside of the ghetto.

Since the process of growth takes place as a reaction to the patterns and priorities of the larger white community, institutional growth and change in the black ghetto is a by-product of such forces rather than a result of more "natural" internal change within the black community itself. Organizational forms, the very scale and scope of organized activity (for example, block clubs versus corporations), emphasize the lack of isomorphic or parallel bases of contact between black communities and the larger urban system.

In essence the ghetto boundary is a membrane that is easily permeable in one direction—influences raining in—but is opaque or far less permeable in the other direction—reaching out for resources. Blacks neither control the major economic institutions of the community nor determine its rhythm of operations. Thus a study by Donald Deskins on the journey-to-work pattern of black and white workers within Detroit from 1953 to 1965 shows that, in the principal occupational groups, the mean distance from home to place of work has steadily increased for blacks and remained constant for whites.[26]

From the opposite side of the border relationship we find that the role of block clubs in preserving racial integration—exchange at the boundary of the ghetto—has served instead as a signal to whites of neighborhood decline. Moreover, as they have proliferated within the central areas of the black ghetto, these same local structures serve as prototypical expressions of community organization—a centripetal rather than a centrifugal force for community development.

Ghettoization for blacks tends to be a process which leads to a kind of premature closure of what types of organizational forms to build, what linkages must be severed with the nonghetto community, and how to protect the cultural and human resources of its inhabitants. In human service organizations, for example, social welfare services in particular have increasingly become black dominated. These are institutional areas which respond to the needs of the local community and provide the social mobility opportunities for the minority of professionally trained blacks living in ghettoes. But at the same they permit the more primary and secondary economic institutions of the society to remain less threatened by black employment and promotion pressures —giving just enough time for such structures to sever their market and territorial links with black population centers. This kind of trade-off or exchange between the black ghetto and the larger white society is a typical instance of the dynamic by which traditional patterns of exchange across "boundaries" has occurred. The autonomy and "separatism" which the ghetto will eventually obtain is being exemplified in the declining centers of cities.

The Compression Model of the Black Ghetto: Key Propositions

We have taken the perspective of human ecology, the spatial and demographic facts of a community's life, and have suggested principles of black ghetto formation and preservation. Let us now move to the specific expressions of these concepts. Each of the subsequent statements may be treated as operational or social indicators of the ghettoization process—in fact, they formed the general hypotheses which guided our research design in the Detroit area. They include the following:

1. Black population concentrations in urban areas represent "artificially" created geographical units characterized by spatial compression and selective growth at the periphery—a product of legal and de facto racial discrimination.

This most fundamental definition is a summary of much of our discussion of ecological dynamics. As such, it serves less as a discrete proposition about the consequences of ghettoization than as a base line. From this fact of black urban life we may then proceed to show the ramifications throughout the social structure of the black ghetto.

2. The spatial attributes and social compression of black population concentrations define patterns of formal as well as informal organizational patterns.

This is a generic statement about the pervasive role of ghettoization. It places the thrust of our argument within the domain of group life in the black ghetto rather than in individual attitudes, beliefs, or perceptions. Both primary community structures, local voluntary associations and patterns of social stratification, become linked in significance as a function of the social forces shaping ghetto life.

3. The spatial/social compression of black population concentrations is associated with significantly more central roles for such social institutions as local neighborhoods and voluntary associations than in other populations.

Here, put into a capsule form, is a central theme of subsequent discussion and elaboration, a major basis for indicating the uniqueness of black ghettoes. Put in its comparative form, the statement points to the differences we expect to find in how individuals use their immediate neighborhood—the functions it performs for them, the role it plays in their life. The same is true for membership in various groups and associations. But once again we must stress the key thesis of our analysis: the particular structure of the black ghetto differs from other parts of the urban community.

4. Where spatial/social compression exists as a major factor in the life of a population, individuals find themselves more often in proximity and social interaction with persons who—while sharing the same perceived attributes of the community—in fact differ in many cases by status level, values, life styles, and other nonascriptive ways.

This statement as applied to the social differentiation of black urban ghettoes introduces the whole theme of social class and its consequences. This proposition particularly calls for an almost opposite perspective from that which commonly ascribes to the black ghetto a sameness and homogeneity of groupings. It is in the diversity of life within the black ghetto that some of the most important social processes are to be understood. Nor is it simply a matter of saying that there are more distinct social class groups in the black ghetto as compared to the white community, although it may be valuable to take this view. More in line with our own perspective is the argument that ghettoization itself may prevent the crystallization of clear social strata and that this very amorphousness in class structure is a key attribute of black ghetto life.

5. Under conditions of spatial/social compression the heightened role of local neighborhoods and voluntary associations enhances status conflict, reduces consensus based on shared values, and increases the isolation of individuals from wider spheres of social participation.

Here we begin the process of tying together the various discrete processes we have described and finally argue for their effects at the individual level. If indeed different socioeconomic groups tend to have some interests in common, the expression of these "class interests" becomes an important basis for what the French sociologist, Emile Durkheim, called "organic" solidarity in a community—the linking of people in their diverse roles through a set of relationships that recognizes the validity of these differences. By contrast simpler and smaller societies, according to Durkheim, can be kept cohesive merely by "mechanical" solidarity—the face-to-face shared norms and social controls that imply virtually no differences between members of the community.

The process by which individuals and groups seek to adapt their actions to the realities of ghetto life produces specific structural patterns. This implies:

> 6. Where the functions of neighborhoods and voluntary associations take on greater significance in a spatially and socially compressed population, a process of structural modification in these institutions tends to take place.

Included in these adaptive responses may be the restricting of memberships in a group to retain its internal cohesion, based on the similarity of outlook of its members. Or a group may seek to respond to the heterogeneity of its potential constituency by altering its formal structure or changing its goals to avoid those productive of dissent.

> 7. Where spatial/social compression characterizes a population, networks of social participation—formal and informal—tend to follow local territorial groupings and this in turn ties individuals to local areas or excludes them once participation goes beyond that immediate territorial arena.

Here we are suggesting a form of dual community structure. For individuals who are locked into the informal web of a neighborhood in the black ghetto, their participation may exclude them from larger centers of participation. And the reverse will also occur. The mutual exclusiveness of the "local" versus the "cosmopolitan" community activist results from the poor linkage between neighborhoods and the outer society. Thus individuals are only able to overcome this bifurcation if they are at the very top of community leadership roles. The ghetto, by its very complexity of status and leadership levels—one system based on territorial commitment, another derived from the educational and occupational differences between local residents—draws the individual into a totally separate sphere of social participation. We shall develop this argument in subsequent chapters. Chart 1 provides a schematic summary of the conceptual model as developed in our research.

CHART 1

Schematic Representation of Ghetto Social Structural Processes

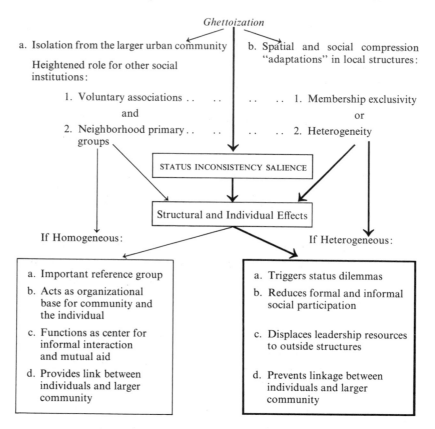

We shall pursue each of the major points enumerated in this part of our discussion—they will serve as guiding formulations for the interpretation of research findings based on the Detroit area study of twenty-eight black and white neighborhoods. Each derives from the overarching model of ghetto social dynamics and in this way forms a test of that construct. Chart 1 schematically depicts the relationships we have been discussing. As a set of interrelated hypotheses about black ghetto communities, they may be taken as separate dimensions or as a set of components all of which must be true. We prefer the first interpretation—a set of separate consequences of ghettoization which may be traced in the life of any one of the larger black population centers. We have initially tested these ideas in Detroit, but we feel they apply to all black ghettoes.

The thrust of our analysis is that black urban populations are organized in response to past and present forces which have often been grasped intuitively but never placed in overall perspective. A sociological formulation about the nature of the ghetto provides a means to step back from the different immediate concerns of the social planner, governmental administrator, community activist, or simply the experiences of the community member with an active interest in the dynamics of his milieu. Our approach does not rest on the treatment of social structure as a sociological abstraction but as a meaningful basis on which to evaluate and define social policies.

Chapter III

The Significance of Social Stratification
for Black Ghettoes

The constricted opportunities and the racially determined limits of the rewards available to the ghetto tend to intensify petty status competitiveness and suspiciousness in the ghetto.

> Kenneth Clark,
> *Dark Ghetto*
> (New York: Harper & Row, 1965), p. 196

The differences between Negro and White community life cannot be measured solely by variations in income, occupation, education and other objective indices. In assessing the differences, it is important to recognize that the Negro class structure and institutions have emerged in response to segregation and represent adjustments to the isolation under which Negroes have lived.

> G. Franklin Edwards,
> "Communities and Class Realities: The Ordeal of Change,"
> *Daedulus*, XCV, 1 (Winter 1966), p. 16

DECAY, UNEMPLOYMENT, AND POVERTY are readily conjured up as images of the black ghetto. But in seeking to understand these realities, the litany of statistical averages purporting to measure them often reduces rather than enhances precision. More dangerous even is the manufacture of false theories growing out of such "averages." Included here are the myths about black families having no cohesion,[1] emphasis on anomic neighborhoods, matriarchy, the inability to defer gratification, and a host of others. In fact what has characterized much of the social science approach to the "black experience," according to a recent critique, is a pattern in which "white sociologists are prone to view the black experience as deviation from traditional, accepted norms in white society. . . . Black sociologists on the other hand are tempted to function as apologists for the black experience and explain and justify its adjudged deviation."[2]

The descriptions and dialogue about black institutions are misleading because the "deviations" of the ghetto effectively mask any analysis of variability. Nowhere is this tendency more evident than in regard to understanding black social stratification. Much of the literature by black and white scholars is critique on the "black bourgeoisie"[3] or "black Anglo-Saxons"[4] or the "lower class culture."[5] In fact no serious empirical study of black ghetto social classes has ever been conducted. Those analyses which are rich in description, such as the work by Drake and Cayton in *Black Metropolis*, have not been updated and are at best highly selective efforts.

The problem of understanding black stratification is that stereotypes of the black ghetto prevent a focus upon wide internal diversity. The preoccupation with "lower class" income, education, and occupational patterns impedes any full comprehension of black ghetto differentiation. We are not speaking merely of rich and poor often living "cheek by jowl" in black neighborhoods, although that is an important reality of ghetto life. We refer as well to the fact that standards of life style and social class may be more diverse and elaborate in black than in white communities. Unfortunately, the specifically spatial aspects of ghetto social stratification, the differences between and within local neighborhoods, is a neglected topic. Full comprehension of ghetto stratification also involves comparing definitions of social class to see whether they fit together in a neatly meshing system or whether they are independent of one another. All of these facets of black stratification need to be explored. Each has tended to be lost in the welter of official statistics and "averages."

Enumerating Social Levels

The study of social stratification has often meant an examination of how many different and distinct social classes exist in a given community or population. Initially such efforts used a single index, such as level of income, but subsequently attempts were made to develop indices composed of several constituent elements. The work of August Hollingshead[6] and W. Lloyd Warner[7] in the 1940s and 1950s exemplifies this basic approach. Thus one question raised in these studies of small and medium sized white communities is: "does a given community have three social classes, or six, or some other number?"

Each "stratum" within the population is seen to have a separate identifiable existence, marked off from other "classes" above and below it. Class in this American sociology approach means a group of persons sharing values, life styles, and socioeconomic level.[8]

How valid is this sort of concept when applied to the black ghetto? In their pioneering work, Drake and Cayton used a three-class system in which life style was a critical basis of differences. As implied in many of the studies on white populations, their analysis defined a pyramid of social classes. In this sense the largest group, the "lower class" is lowest in status. In describing the "system of social classes in Bronzeville (Chicago)" Drake and Cayton state that "everybody in Bronzeville recognizes the existence of social classes, whether called that or not."[9] One of the hints that such a neat "class hierarchy" does not fit well with the reality of ghetto life is that Drake and Cayton divide the "lower class" into a "church-oriented group," "shadies," and the "underworld." In a later discussion St. Clair Drake describes the black middle class as "merely a collection of people who have similar life styles and aspirations, whose basic goals are 'living well' being 'respectable' and not being crude."[10]

Subjective Criteria of Social Class. One of the major points made about black stratification is that on "objective" grounds (using criteria such as educational, occupational, and income levels) racial discrimination produces a skewed distribution. Blacks are not able to manifest the full range of advance on these indices and the result is a "compression" of the social ladder. Studies such as the analysis by Drake and Cayton, and more recently the work of Billingsley on black families, suggest that "subjective" class criteria are better measures of black stratification. Essentially the argument is that since socioeconomic level is distorted by discrimination, unique and internally valid definitions arise from the life of the ghetto. These include extent of participation in organizations, and "respectability."

Still other writers have been brought to the view that when "white" (socioeconomic levels) criteria of stratification are applied to a black population, there they are not likely to be very useful. Thus, Jay Williams[11] in reviewing the major studies of white psychological personality dynamics as related to social class position, finds that when these same factors are utilized in the study of a black population the predicted difference simply did not occur. In other words, a middle class white person may be distinguished in terms of particular attitudes and values with regards to marriage, work, political behavior, and religious attitudes. There are no similar correlates among the black population.

The failure of various indices of white stratification to predict validly the behavior of individual blacks has lead some researchers to argue that in fact there may be other criteria that are intrinsic to the black ghetto, which serve as a completely separate system of stratification. As Williams states, "the failure . . . to organize the data deepened the mystery of what factors could be successfully included in an index to organize Negro data . . . in looking for the answer to the riddle of Negro social class, cultural variables are of prime importance. . . ."[12]

There is yet a further implication to be drawn from questioning the applicability of existing stratification studies to the black ghetto. It takes the form of a caveat: "ignore such factors as income, education, and occupation because these are fundamentally defined by the larger white society." Instead this argument suggests in order to comprehend the subtlety and significance of status in the black community we must look within it for those kinds of evaluations that one black person makes of another. Only then do we become aware of the "true" dimensions of social status and class.

The problem with the argument for a separate cultural determination of stratification is that, first of all, it assumes that all social class systems are somehow merely the product of perceived realities and that there is no objective basis for such stratification. But it is of fundamental significance to recognize that the economic and social position of blacks living in a ghetto is, in fact, not independent of the larger white society. And this is not merely the issue of whether blacks accept the status rankings which whites utilize. Rather that when we objectively look at the structure of black communities we find that the individuals who live in that setting have resources both economic and educational which are a function of the interplay of the black ghetto with the larger white society. Therefore in searching for any significant bases to describe stratification in the black ghetto we must somehow take account of the reality of the larger society.

How can we approach social class in the black ghetto if it tends to have a combination of objective and subjective meanings? Caution in the applicability of "white standards" coupled with somewhat unique "cultural" definitions emanating from ghetto life itself make the counting of social strata difficult if not futile. As a result, understanding black stratification in the sense of discrete social classes may result in more complex models than are needed in a white community context or may require the total abandonment of the "layer cake" approach.

Reference Groups: A Further Variation of the Status Complexity Theme.   If social classes are segments of society with which individuals tend to identify themselves and which follow particular behavior patterns, then we can broaden this idea to include any point of reference that individuals may use to define their own position in their community and society. The sociological term "reference group" then refers to a perceived position that one holds in a group which is a yardstick for measuring one's own and others' behavior.

Thus we can talk about guiding our behavior by the patterns of those groups to which we aspire, even though we may not actually belong to them. At the same time we can think about the idea that individuals who might be considered "lower class" in some sense may have "middle class" values.

This kind of split between membership group and reference group has been widely commented upon in modern sociology. It is clear that we cannot easily predict the behavior of individuals simply by knowing their membership group. Instead we must also know which groups the individual uses as a standard for judging his own position. Merely being a member of the working class does not mean that the individual identifies as a worker. A white-collar professional may have an extensive formal education, but may view himself as a member of a radical and militant group promoting the causes of the working man. Blacks living in urban ghettoes may find as their close neighbors individuals whose educational level is so sharply different from their own that contact only intensifies the differentiation.[13]

We know very little about how individuals form reference groups, but clearly to the extent that individuals find themselves interacting in face-to-face situations, there is a tendency for individuals to seek out those who share common values and attitudes. A common basis of experience becomes an important way by which individuals signal the fact that they share similar interests. To be attached to a social group may at the same time require that one isolate oneself from others in the immediate environment who do not fit the same standards of values and attitudes. Merely having ready contact or being in an area of proximity with others does not determine what the reference group may be.

Geography and Ghetto Stratification. The discussion of class levels in the traditional literature of sociology frequently describes or often implies that territorial patterns express stratum boundaries. In this sense, local neighborhoods are inextricably bound up with definitions of social class. But our discussion of reference groups in the black ghetto has implied that physical proximity may be an indicator of special dynamics in the black versus white neighborhood setting.

If the housing patterns of blacks are a product of white exodus, is it correct to see the local neighborhood as a basis of black social stratification? First of all, the physical compression of the black ghetto results in a far greater potentiality of contact between persons who rank differently on a single status indicator than occurs in typical white communities. In other words, a high school principal and a political leader may find themselves living in the same neighborhood with the unskilled blue-collar worker or the ADC mother. Glazer and Moynihan in describing this pattern state that "the Negro middle class . . . rarely escapes from the near presence of the Negro poor, as well as the depraved and the criminal. The middle class neighborhoods border on the lower class neighborhoods, and suffer from robberies and attacks and the psychic assaults of a hundred awful sights."[14]

In our Detroit study we had a chance to measure the dynamics of physical setting as they reflected the concept of reference group. Thus, as we were observing the character of internal and external housing decorations of the various neighborhoods in which we carried out the study, we found that in white neighborhoods there tended to be a pattern to the decorative additions to houses. These seemed to be quite uniform on a given block. For instance, the gaslight lamp-post, which was a frequent accessory in many middle class or lower middle class homes, tended to be rather uniformly introduced on a given block where residents were white. When we examined this same pattern as it occurred in black ghetto neighborhoods, a different distribution was frequently found. In this case there tended to be a more separate use of the external gaslight lamp-post. In other words, black residents in relatively few instances had the same lamp-post in terms of houses that were clustered near one another. Just as often these lamp-posts tended to be scattered on a fairly wide distribution throughout a given block, rather than being uniformly clustered.

What do these differences suggest? In terms of the overall analysis they seem to imply that for whites the external decoration of the home was a sign of conformity. In other words, the housing pattern of a given block tended to represent not just a membership group but also a reference group. By contrast, for black residents, the scattered pattern suggested that the lamp-post was really not a way to conform but instead to differentiate oneself from neighbors. The reference group might be formed by those residents who would signal each other literally in terms of displaying the lamp-post.

This is but one instance of how social participation patterns tend to reflect a desire to maximize the extent of participation in common membership and reference groups. But what happens when the two are split, when individuals live in neighborhoods where there are relatively few members of their own reference group? This may result in a withdrawal of participation in that setting or a greater cost in time, space, and energy exerted in order to make contact with those who *are* members of the reference group but who reside outside of the local neighborhoods.

Individuals who find themselves in settings where they cannot automatically assume that those around them share common values may be wary of engaging in social interaction until some signal has been provided by the other person or some clear set of symbols has been exchanged. Thus it may be that some of the stress that minority group members place on visible symbols of status (automobiles, clothing, etc.), is a necessary function of ghetto life. For individuals to signal to others about their common interest it may be necessary to have very clearly visible flags thrown up which suggest, in fact, to which reference group that person belongs in a context where race is a given.

A Critical Dynamic: Inconsistency of Status in the Ghetto

In our discussion of black stratification we have described a set of different factors which share an underlying characteristic—they all relate to status blurring. In the case of unclear social class dividing lines we may plausibly argue that there is no set of uniform criteria of stratification which finds complete application in the black ghetto. "Borrowing" social class concepts from whites represents artificial strata or at least adds elements which make stratification more complex. In turn, our discussion of neighborhood patterns means that identification of individual status is made more difficult because residential areas have greater status differences contained within them.

Yet all the points we have made add up to the view that social status in the ghetto is more elusive than in the white community. "Crystallization" of one's social rank is therefore a more difficult task to achieve in the black ghetto. Individuals who may on one criteria appear to be upper middle class, let us say level of formal education, may in terms of income be lower middle class. At the same time, the number of individuals whose occupational sphere is such that their status would rank fairly low may indeed have incomes which are moderate or even relatively affluent. Here we are speaking about the skilled blue-collar workers whose position both in the black and white community tends to be one that places them at the same level as many white-collar professionals in terms of income, but whose life styles and values differ markedly because of differences in educational levels.

In Detroit we were able to introduce a series of analyses which examine how objective socioeconomic criteria predicted various kinds of behaviors. We were also able to gather data on the extent to which individuals found themselves in a situation where their ranking on one indicator of status differed sharply from their ranking on another. This concept, which is referred to in the stratification literature as "status inconsistency,"[15] becomes a fundamental way to try to describe the dynamics which characterize the black ghetto. Thus, the status inconsistent person is someone who may well have shown social mobility on one indicator (such as family income), but whose educational level or occupational position tends to lag behind.

What are the specific implications of such rankings for the behavior of individuals? In the Detroit study we found a series of correlates of "status inconsistency" as they operated in the black population as compared to the white population. One of the best examples of these findings has to do with a series of attitudes which has generally been labeled "anomie." The research utilized a series of questions which asked the interviewees whether they felt they could trust others, whether public officials cared what they thought, whether they felt that a person has to live pretty much for today and let tomorrow take care of itself, and whether they often felt lonely. Using the scale and taking the social class indicators of income, education, and occupation, those individuals in the white community who were consistent across the different indicators were found to have an increasingly greater sense of anomie the lower they were on these indicators.

But when we examine the black population concentrated in Detroit's urban ghetto we find a totally different pattern. The traditional social class indicators do not give us a good prediction of whether black people will have attitudes of anomie.[16] Instead it is the extent of *inconsistency* between these indicators which proves to be the greater source of predicting about anomie (see Appendix, table 1A). In other words, in the black ghetto it is far less important in understanding the attitudes of anomie to know whether the person is consistently low on education, income, and occupation than to know whether the individual has a relatively high rank on one of these indicators versus a relatively low rank on another. The predictor of attitudes turns out to be not the uniformity of social class rankings, but rather their diversity.

Our Detroit study indicates that inconsistency of status among blacks is related to participating in different ways in both the local neighborhood and in other organizations. Those whose income, education, or job does not fit the typical pattern of their neighbors often join groups where neighbors are not members. Those whose status is inconsistent using the standards of the total black group surveyed, often have a high level of participation in their local neighborhood but avoid being active beyond the confines of that immediate environment. Status inconsistents in the black ghetto have a major role to play in terms of their generally higher level of joining groups and in the special patterns which that participation takes on (see Appendix, table 2A).

The Detroit findings do not indicate that status inconsistency is present in the black ghetto but absent in the white community. In fact, using a purely statistical approach it is easier for a white individual to become inconsistent given the wider variations in income, education, and job that may occur. At this point the reader might well ask: "isn't it true that, contrary to the important fact of status inconsistency among blacks living in the ghetto, most of its residents tend to be low in education, low in income, and low in occupational rank?" This is certainly a disturbing truth about the present condition of black Americans in urban centers. But the fact remains that in spite of what one would anticipate to be the degree of uniformity in black ghettoes it is the extent of *heterogeneity* which has to be explained.

In other words, given the economic positions of blacks in American cities, we would expect that the character of urban ghettoes should be one of extreme homogeneity. But the countervailing force in regard to the social structure of the black ghetto is the restricted residential mobility of the more affluent members of the black population. Thus in the case of the Detroit study we find that in terms of income about 1 out of 2 whites had income levels exceeding $10,000 as compared with only 3 out of 10 blacks; in terms of education, about one-fourth of the white population had gone beyond high school education compared to only 1 out of 7 blacks; and finally, in terms of occupational levels, 1 out of 3 whites were in white-collar jobs compared to 1 out of 6 blacks. Yet for those individuals whose ranks on either income or education or occupation differed, the proportions of these groups in the white and black samples were virtually identical. In other words, irrespective of the heavy concentration of blacks in the lower socioeconomic level, the extent to which individuals in the black community were likely to be status inconsistent was as great as it was in the white sample. Moreover, where such patterns occur in the black ghetto setting, our analysis indicates that its significance is more apparent for a wide range of individual factors of behavior and attitudes than in a population of white individuals (see Appendix, table 3A).

Status and the Institutional Life of the Neighborhood. Fundamental to our discussion of stratification has been the view that ghettoization creates restricted residential movement. As a result, the social mobility experienced by a portion of the black community is not readily translated into residential mobility. The character of neighborhoods into which the more affluent black person may move will be determined in part by the exodus of whites. Moreover, the existence of a tightly organized community focused on a compacted area of social interaction means that the institutional focus of the black community is often tied to neighborhoods. In other words, organizations, friendship patterns, and informal groupings of all kinds are more likely to find their sphere of influence spatially limited to a greater extent than in the white community. The result of this is to create a seeming paradox: on the one hand social class is less clearly defined in the black ghetto, but at the same time it is much more often delimited by a physical setting. This paradox implies that the local neighborhood often serves as a center for defining a person's social class position. As we have already noted, the symbols of social status may tend to be localized in the residential neighborhood. This may include housing, automobile styles, and other readily visible external trappings of status.

Conflicting with the need to define one's status in terms of the local arena is the heterogeneity which may characterize black residential areas. Thus it is more difficult to assume that one's status peers are going to be found in close proximity than for a nonghetto resident.

The concentration of black populations in physically demarcated areas results in a greater degree of blurring of social class lines within the black ghetto. The result is to create a multiplicity of reference groups which may not be synonymous with the physical setting in which people reside. The "natural" linkage, then, between physical setting and social position tends to be minimized in the black ghetto. We cannot therefore discuss social class in the black community in terms of the highly crystallized patterns which tend to characterize white communities. There is great social differentiation in the black community but it does not appear to be coherently focused in discrete groups, or of discretely located middle class versus lower class versus working class neighborhoods. This tends to undermine the "class solidarity" of a neighborhood. Moreover, it makes it more difficult for those with the specialized skills needed to achieve local action goals to feel identified with their residential area. Black professionals may not be able to find a sufficient number of status peers in their neighborhood. They may belong to many professional groups but meet few neighbors in these organizations. The result is a kind of "displacement" of expertise and leadership out of the local milieu.

The assurance that local neighborhood institutions tend to reflect the natural status groupings of a community simply does not exist in the ghettoized community. This is true because the inherited physical patterns of neighborhoods are not a natural outgrowth of stratification expressed in terms of voluntary choice of residence, but instead are the result of the structures imposed by housing segregation. The manifestation of that process in the internal life of the black ghetto often means that individuals are confronted with a difficult choice in deciding whether or not to participate: if I focus my interest on the local neighborhood, this brings me into contact with individuals who may not share my life styles or values, even though we have an ethnic identification. The white individual is far less frequently faced with such a choice. For blacks in the ghetto, status contradictions are liable to determine community participation in ways not readily seen to enhance cohesion for that community.

In terms of such groups as PTAs, or the local school itself, the pattern of black neighborhood status differences translates into greater problems of consensus around such matters as curriculum and school goals. Whereas the white school administrator can more often presume that "politics" are submerged by the "natural" consensus of the local area, his or her black counterpart may have to deal more overtly with creating common values and priorities. Many black ghetto organizations may be confronted with this task. Its origins are the patterns of stratification built into neighborhoods and groups which must accommodate a wider range of differences in outlook and social status. Coping with such problems may deflect the group from its original activities. Tensions and interpersonal clashes may be manifestation of the essentially "structural" sources of confrontation due to status diversities. The mechanisms by which a local school, a local organization, or block club is able to take account of this diversity are crucial for their effectiveness.

Given the greater role of the local neighborhood community in the black ghetto, status conflicts within that sphere have consequences which are far-reaching in terms of a wide range of social goals. If individuals find themselves focusing exclusively on their local neighborhood because the larger institutions in the black ghetto are costly to utilize, both in terms of time and distance, then it becomes an especially important problem for such individuals to utilize their local neighborhood as a viable community.

Class versus Community. For the advocate of radical action as well as the supporter of more moderate efforts toward change in the black ghetto, confrontation with the realities and social class dynamics in the black community is fundamental. The fact of unique status diversity in the ghetto tends to be inconsistent with the demands for an increasing unity and positive self-image among blacks in urban areas. One of the most urgent and necessary elements of any program of black unity is to insure that the multiplicity of status groups represented in the ghetto is maintained in some fundamental linkage as a community. With the growing evidence that affluent blacks as well as whites have been moving rapidly out of central cities the specter is suggested that the diversity of ghetto life which presents a special problem in black unity may give way to a homogeneity often assumed already to exist in the black community. Thus, the task becomes how to integrate all members of the black community in coherent and effective common interests, but at the same time to recognize the dilemmas presented by a ghettoized way of life.

Reviewing Key Stratification Issues of the Ghetto

We need at this point to summarize the major points that we have made. First of all, (1) We have argued that the traditional notion of social stratification, which is an outgrowth of white sociological analysis, may not apply to the black ghetto. (2) We have substituted for the notion of discrete social classes the concept that black ghetto residents are differentiated by socioeconomic status but that the consistency of these ranks tends often to be extremely variable. (3) The result is that social class lines tend to be blurred in the black ghetto. As a result of the blurring, other criteria of social class may emerge and take on greater significance than they would in the white community. Here we may be speaking of the particular symbols of status, patterns of consumption, and other forms of "cultural" intrusions into the objective criteria of status which may take on special importance in the black community. (4) We have suggested that the local neighborhood may be a particularly salient arena of status, given the relative isolation and exclusion that many ghetto inhabitants experience vis-à-vis the larger institutions of the white society. (5) We have indicated that there are likely to be dilemmas present where blacks have experienced a degree of affluence and have moved into reference group orientations of job, education, or life-style which cannot be associated with an immediate area of residential location. (6) We have described in terms of several forces of social diversity what appears to be an expression of black ghetto growth and the complexity of stratification which is manifested in comparison with white communities. (7) We have suggested that the status dynamics of the black community play a fundamental role in the institutional life of the black ghetto. (8) We have indicated that in the larger considerations of strategy and policy-making the design for social change must go beyond considerations of blacks controlling white governmental structures of the local community and becoming policy-makers within the existing institutions of central cities, but that these gains may require a reexamination of the institutional arrangements which were predicated upon a community whose growth patterns were reflective of a greater degree of homogeneity within its population than can ever be found for any black population concentration in America's urban centers.

Chapter IV

Local Neighborhoods and the Structure
of the Black Ghetto

Even the most distinctive "natural areas" of cities (those with homogeneous populations, a historic identity, strong social traditions, and considerable stability) cannot
escape the pressure toward ceaseless and rapid movement and heterogeneity that trans-
forms these neighborhoods into hybrid creatures suspended between past and future.

> Suzanne Keller,
> *The Urban Neighborhood: A Sociological Perspective*
> (New York: Random House, 1968), p. 12

In some populations it is reasonable to assume that people can and do remain heavily
engrossed in their local neighborhood as a separate and rather distinct moral world. . . .
Localisms of this type simply increase the degree of social differentiation and provide
an additional basis for association.

> Gerald Suttles,
> *The Social Order of the Slum*
> (Chicago: University of Chicago Press, 1968), p. 5

DURING THE 1950s a great deal of social science literature was
developed around the theme of America as a mass society. In the next
decade the local community was "rediscovered." Federal programs
dealing with poverty emphasized the neighborhood concept. More
recently the movement toward "local control" and "neighborhood
government" has signalled an even greater focus on the viability of
local residential areas as basic social systems.

The "Chicago school" sociologists of the 1920s spoke of neighborhoods as "natural areas" marked off by differences in social class
and ethnicity and by physical barriers.[1] Recent studies have cast
doubt on this approach and suggest the wide range of ways neighborhoods are perceived and the role they play in the lives of individual
urban dwellers. In this perspective there is no point in trying to define
the boundaries of such units since social and physical groupings do not
necessarily nor often coincide.[2] In the words of one sociologist, it may

be more important to "consider the social relationships themselves than to worry about where neighborhoods begin and end."[3]

The difficulty in demonstrating that spatial and social dimensions of the neighborhood are really part of the same phenomenon has resulted in many social scientists separating the two concepts. On the one hand neighborhood is treated as a mere "reference group"—a social-psychological construct of the mind; on the other hand some researchers continue to describe the neighborhood as a key "social area."[4]

Our approach is to eschew this dichotomy and focus on the neighborhood in terms of a question of the following kind: What is the function of this local community? Are neighborhoods important, and if they are, in what ways? The suggestion that the concept of "neighborhood" might contribute significantly to the explanation of what a community is, directly contradicts a significant portion of the literature regarding the modern industrial state according to which the neighborhood, like all other primary groups, such as the family and friendship cliques, has lost significance in the face of large-scale bureaucratic structures. This belief in the demise of the neighborhood as an important social unit, is predicated upon the assumption that the neighborhood is exclusively a primary group and therefore should possess the "face-to-face," intimate, affective relations which characterize all primary groups. It would appear, then, given the validity of this notion, that many urban communities have moved away from this form of social organization.

Mitigating against the rejection of the neighborhood as a useful concept is the fact that numerous studies continue to affirm that the neighborhood is an important force in shaping individual behavior. Sussman and White, for example, in a study carried out in 1959, found that anonymity and impersonality, believed to exist among people living in the same urban areas, did *not* in fact exist. Nearly all of their sample knew at least one neighbor, while at least half knew four or more neighbors.[5] Herbert Gans' classic study of Boston's West End, *The Urban Villagers*,[6] offers an important rebuttal to those who declare that the neighborhood is dead as an important concept. A similar study, by Gerald Suttles in 1968, of neighborhoods occupied by four different ethnic groups in Chicago also confirms the thesis that the neighborhood is a living and vital force in the lives of many urban inhabitants.[7] Studies by Litwak and his colleagues continue to support the contention that the neighborhood is an important force in terms of individual social mobility.[8]

Defining Neighborhood

The first problem encountered in any effort to synthesize present knowledge about the urban neighborhood is the existence of varied and inconsistent definitions of the term "neighborhood." At times it refers to an area with commonly recognized physical properties, or again it refers to a set of comparatively intimate and permanent human activities and relationships defined by such terms as "primary group" or "neighborliness." This confounding of spatial and social dimensions has obscured important ways to distinguish one neighborhood process from another.

A major problem arising from the spatial referent concerns the precise delimiting of neighborhood boundaries. In some studies, high school districts are said to be neighborhoods. In other studies, an acknowledged subcommunity such as Greenwich Village is thought of as a neighborhood. Caplow and Foreman employed as a working definition of neighborhood in Minneapolis-St. Paul "a family dwelling unit and the ten family dwelling units most accessible to it."[9] Judith Shuval, in a study of Israeli ethnic groups, defined a "micro-neighborhood" as one composed of three families, the respondent's and those of his two closest neighbors.[10] Shimon Spiro utilized the same definition in speaking of the "nuclear neighborhood."[11] Scott Greer, in studying the problem of the size of neighborhood units, defines four different levels: (1) the household; (2) the neighborhood; (3) the local area of residence; and (4) the municipality.[12]

In Detroit we utilized in our research a concept of neighborhood which focused on the elementary school district as an appropriate unit of what local community means to most urban dwellers.

Mechanisms of Neighborhood Influence

Although the size and organization of neighborhoods suggests the diversity of social units, it is possible to reduce the means by which the neighborhood influences the lives of individuals to three processes which are often inter-related. One of these, "selective recruitment," involves administrative decisions of public agencies that lead to particular kinds of people locating in a given area or the process by which a neighborhood encourages particular kinds of families or individuals to move there. Welfare families, for example, might be located adjacent to one another or closer to service centers, public housing projects, etc. Or there might be a kind of "self-selection" based on a perceived similarity between oneself and one's potential neighbors. Selective recruitment may operate in a latent fashion, for example, in the pricing of homes or in activities of neighborhood associations that put pressure on residents or real estate agents to sell to the "right people." "Sponsored" recruitment, wherein a new resident already has friends in the neighborhood, is a variation of selective recruitment. In both latent and manifest forms, selective recruitment is probably one of the major ways in which neighborhood homogeneity is fostered. When coupled with governmental housing policies, which cluster specific social groups in specific locales, this process provides an even higher degree of residential segregation—based on social class, race, or ethnicity—which otherwise might not occur.

The second process of neighborhood influence is one of socialization; in other words, persons with specific values or behaviors tend to influence one another as a result of being in proximity and as the consequence of the neighboring process itself.

The third process we can identify is selective expulsion of individuals whose life patterns or values are at odds with that of the neighborhood. In other words, there is a built-in capacity of a local area to punish those who deviate from its patterns and eventually to expel such individuals either directly or indirectly from the area.

The socialization process refers to a range of ways in which newcomers are changed to conform to neighborhood norms. Frequently, socialization operates in conjunction with selective recruitment and expulsion. Selective expulsion may occur when there is an open intake process whereby requirements for income level and other factors provide for effective pruning of residents. Public housing and public schools often create such pruning effects by eliminating various types of deviants from those who are otherwise "qualified" residents of the neighborhood.

All things being equal, the lower the status of the neighborhood, the more likely it is that the group will use selective expulsion rather than selective recruitment. Exceptions to this principle are upwardly mobile people who feel that their neighbors are not suitable peer groups and who try to isolate themselves in preparation for leaving the neighborhood. This is referred to as "self-selective expulsion."

Self-selective expulsion and "group expulsion" may go hand in hand. To the extent that local neighborhoods are key social units in a community these processes become basic sociological forces.

Special Functions of Neighborhood in a Mass Society

The central issue confronting the student of urban communities is the question of whether local neighborhoods are important enough to warrant special study, either for theoretical or practical reasons. It has been argued, that with the advent of urbanization and bureaucratization, neighborhoods are declining in significance along with other primary groups. Many researchers see the suburban community as the repository for the neighborliness and intensive social action that once reputedly existed in core city neighborhoods. Thus, suburban living may represent an entirely different way of life from the city, and the high degree of suburban sociability may be evidence of such a distinct pattern.

A major factor for variation in the degree to which neighborhoods are centers for social interaction is the degree of homogeneity. It has been argued that homogeneity is not a significant basis for neighborhood cohesion when the external social institutions of education and mass communication reduce sharp value differences between persons of different ethnic, racial, and regional backgrounds. In other words, the argument is that in a mass society, most of our attitudes are shaped by our educational level and our exposure to information coming from outside of the local neighborhood.

One difficulty in sorting out the findings on the role of the neighborhood is the reliance on a sort of "ideal" cohesive and homogeneous area where social intimacy and exclusive primary group ties are maintained under conditions of low population turnover. Such a setting is clearly not evident in most neighborhoods in medium sized or large cities. On the other hand, the totally disorganized or anomic residential area seems to be also equally atypical.

In research by Litwak and Szelenyi[13] there is a suggestion that, even in a highly industrialized society, three factors provide the neighborhood with a unique set of functions. The first is the speed of reaction possible between neighbors in dealing with special or common problems. These problems may include such things as health emergencies, the need to borrow the proverbial "cup of sugar," or a range of other problems where the actual proximity of neighbors becomes the crucial factor in providing aid. The second is the special services based on common territorial needs, including the local school, certain kinds of social services that are provided to a neighborhood, and the fact that most statistics gathered on populations to determine their needs have an "administrative" definition of neighborhood. This may be the police precinct, the health district, the census tract, etc. The third factor is the face-to-face contact that creates highly visible effects on social behavior, such as child rearing and children's educational performance. A local neighborhood becomes a kind of testing ground for most of the definitions of what is and what is not socially acceptable.

There are six functions of neighborhoods that can be defined as potentially operating in a local area. We shall discuss briefly each of these and point out their significance, both for the individual and for the total community. The extent to which at least one, or more often, several of these functions are prevalent in a given local area then becomes an empirical question to be investigated.
We can list these as follows:

1. Neighborhood as a center for interpersonal influence.
2. Neighborhood as a source of mutual aid.
3. Neighborhood as an organizational base, both in terms of formal gatherings as well as more informal voluntary associations.
4. Neighborhood as a reference group or a context in which individuals influence each other in indirect ways.
5. Neighborhood as a status arena.
6. Neighborhood as a basis for defining social problems.

Neighborhood as a Center for Interpersonal Influence.   This function of the neighborhood refers to the extent of interaction which occurs between individuals in a neighborhood setting. It includes the "nodding acquaintanceships" which may occur in neighborhoods and the more qualitatively significant and intimate social relationships, wherein close friendships and ties develop and where important social behaviors and values come to be tested and evaluated. Children learn these social behaviors and values through continuous observation and imitation of adult neighbors and peer groups. Forms of social influence such as ostracism or rewards based on social acceptance take on a reality base in the local neighborhood. Thus, immediate information and feedback and the rapid socialization which takes place when face-to-face contacts with neighbors are frequent and intense, provide the means of defining values in such areas as child rearing, education, economic aspirations, political attitudes, and a wide range of areas which have pertinence on one's position and relationship to the larger society.

Political influence in local areas has been analyzed in terms of what is called the "two-step flow" of communications, which points out that the mass media very rarely influence individuals in a purely direct sense. Their influences are mediated through the local contacts one has with so-called opinion leaders.[14] These individuals are knowledgeable about the contents of the media and often filter the ideas of the larger society down to the local level. The classic study of this kind had to do with voting behavior, where it ascertained that individuals who were not tuned in to the media directly, often received their information from local opinion leaders who had a great deal of knowledge about what had been said in campaigns. In Detroit, there was a recent demonstration of the role of this two-step communication process when a shoot-out occurred between Detroit police and black nationalists. This "New Bethel Church Incident" provided an opportunity to demonstrate that when individuals in the black community listened to the media, they tended not to accept its message about what had occurred and that the sense of right or wrong behavior on the part of the police tended to be determined, in part, by what neighbors and friends said. This "filtering" process became a way to understand how blacks interpret the messages coming from the media.

This same New Bethel study also gives us a hint as to the greater significance of the role of local neighborhoods with respect to the black community. The study showed that an overwhelming majority of white respondents in Detroit accepted the view that the incident involved an "ambush by militants of the police officers." This view, which originally had emerged from television coverage, was very difficult to reverse, and the direct link between whites and the media prevented any real knowledge of what was occurring in the black community. Therefore, the absence of localized contacts with blacks tended to mean a greater willingness to accept a media message.

The filtering role of local opinion leaders provides a mechanism both for integrating the individual into the larger society and for preventing the breakdown of local norms by expurgating ideas which do not conform to that local setting.

The Neighborhood and Mutual Aid. A second very crucial function of the neighborhood in contemporary society is that it serves as a basis for the exchange of help between those living in close proximity. The rapid response of neighbors is crucial when aid is not available from other sources, such as relatives or formal organizations. For example, most studies of disasters show that something close to three-quarters of all disaster rescues are made by neighbors.[15]

Despite the proliferation of welfare agencies, such organizations lack the ability to respond properly and flexibly to emergencies. A study of fatherless families by Kriesberg and Bellin[16] found that mutual aid was extensive for employed mothers of fatherless families, and minor exchanges—borrowing or lending groceries or small amounts of money, babysitting or shopping—were found to be frequent for both husbandless and married mothers. Only 16 percent of the persons interviewed did not report such exchanges.

The local neighborhood role as a center for mutual aid may take the form of protection against outside intrusions as well as a substitute for external support. Gerald Suttles in *The Social Order of the Slum* describes this process among four major ethnic groups, in Chicago where the notion of territorial turf is a central concept in a community. Thus, refusing to give information to authorities or to aid the police or institutions viewed as alien to neighborhood values is an important protective device operating in a given neighborhood. For example, if there is a sudden disaster or when resources must be sought outside the neighborhood or where protection from outside social institutions alien to the local area is involved, mutual aid plays a significant role for many urban families.

Neighborhood as an Organizational Base. Neighborhood participation may: (1) serve as a parallel to participation in wider circles of the community; (2) it may compete with other social units in the community; or (3) it may link with or facilitate participation in the larger community. Participation in the local community may serve as a basis for moving up and out of a neighborhood, and voluntary associations are often used to speed the integration of individuals into the local neighborhood. (William White wrote about this extensively in his discussion of the mobile executive, *The Organization Man.*) The importance of participating in the local community can be a basis for individuals to move quickly into a new job setting. Depending on the types of groups, such as PTAs or similar organizations, they need not conflict with other social units, such as the family, or prevent individuals from forming close, informal ties with their neighbors. In this sense, local organizations, such as block clubs, churches, and other institutions, help to integrate the individual into the neighborhood and into the activities of the larger community. If a neighborhood has a capacity to integrate people quickly, by such institutions as the "Welcome Wagon" or its counterparts, a population which is undergoing turnover need not experience a lack of neighborhood cohesion. However, the argument that voluntary organizations act as links between the isolated individual and the larger social institutions is subject to qualification. Under some circumstances local organizations provide the stimulus to engage in efforts to change society in nonconventional ways. Social movements of a radical kind are as likely to emerge from the alienation of a local neighborhood as from the attachment people may feel to distant symbols of nationalism, religion, or race.

Neighborhood as a Reference Group. Although many studies suggest that informal and formal contacts are extensive in many neighborhoods, the fact that many neighbor contacts are ephemeral and low in intensity suggests that the influence exerted by neighbors is often very subjective. In this sense, a neighborhood is a group in the mind of the beholder, rather than one that is visible because of extensive social interaction. Using the term "reference group," it can be said that individuals may be guided and changed in their behavior and values by what they understand to be the values of a perceived group or entity known as the "neighborhood." In this sense, an individual's self-image may be shaped by what "he thinks others think of him."

The results of several studies have supported the theory that the role of neighborhood effects is based on the overall attributes or the majority values in a given setting.[17] For example, a study on the relationship between the status level of a neighborhood and the delinquency rates of boys at each of several social class levels shows that boys who reside in high status areas have a minimal chance of becoming delinquents, but boys from both wealthy and poor families are more likely to become delinquent in low status areas.[18]

Others have found that the neighborhood influences educational plans and attitudes, apart from the influence of the socioeconomic position of the individual family.[19] In this sense the neighborhood acts as an influence on individuals through an indirect process. The majority of neighbors are perceived to hold certain values. They may transmit norms about appropriate or inappropriate behavior, based on rather minimal contact between neighbors, or more casual and less intense kinds of social patterns than the kind described by opinion leaders or evident in close friendship patterns.

Thus, the social climate of a neighborhood may lead individuals to seek out others who agree with them and thereby reinforce the attitudes they already have. But merely *believing* that a majority of one's neighbors agree with one's views may have the same effect. This "pluralistic ignorance" may be facilitated by the lack of extensive social interaction that makes the urban neighborhood something less than an intimate and primary group setting. *That is, the very absence of contact between neighbors may reinforce an idea of what neighbors believe when in fact this may not be the case.* This concept, which was first described in a classic study of a small New England community, involved the fact that when interviewers asked people whether card games between neighbors and friends involved gambling, each person denied that this was going on outside of his own immediate household.[20] In fact, the interviewers actually found a generalized pattern of this form of behavior.

Thus, individuals may not consciously or directly see themselves as conforming to neighborhood norms, but the characteristics of those living in the neighborhood may produce a set of social forces which guides people toward particular behaviors and attitudes. The very isolation of individuals from one another in urban neighborhoods may serve only to heighten this perceived set of norms. The individuals involved in the gambling viewed themselves as deviating from the behavior of their neighbors. This set up a discrepancy between their willingness to discuss common attitudes and the sense that their projecting such values might run contrary to their neighbors' views.

This is consistent with the classic statement by W. I. Thomas that "if people believe that events are real, then these events are real in their consequences." The more people consider their neighborhood as a reference group, the more likely they are to perceive that there are social forces which function and influence them, but which are not dependent upon a great deal of contact with their neighbors.

The Neighborhood as a Status Arena. Perhaps the least explored function of a neighborhood is its importance as a status-conferring entity. Status symbols, in terms of housing or prestige of living in the neighborhood, and individually developed status definitions granted by neighbors, have been the subject of some research. The neighborhood may act as a mirror of personal achievement and well-being:

1. by screening out definitions of class or status that are valued in the larger society but are irrelevant at the local level;
2. by providing an area within which status claims derived from the larger society can be "cashed in"—in terms of housing, life style, or other highly visible definitions of social position.

In the first instance, the neighborhood serves as a generating source of status claims that may replace those valued by the larger society. In other words, the neighborhood may develop its own criteria for high or low status. As status centers, neighborhoods enable local opinion leaders or other status figures who may be sought out or interacted with to provide "status bestowal and appraisal." For example, when an individual wants to find out whether his particular style of interior house decorating is valued or not, he may check this out with a local neighbor.

People who are themselves "deviant" from the majority often selectively interact with those neighbors whose status position is inconsistent with the general area. Adequate conferral for otherwise locally threatened status may be found. *This suggests that neither the volume of neighbor contacts nor other measures of social participation are adequate indicators of this specific function of the neighborhood.*

In other words, individuals may have a small clique of friends in the local community which represents their particular status arena. This is possible when the neighborhood is extremely diverse in composition. Therefore, one of the important roles of neighborhoods in a highly heterogeneous setting is the status-conferral function. The more heterogeneous the neighborhood, the more necessary it may be to seek out the few status peers in the local area who can provide a basis for defining one's own position.

Neighborhood as a Problem-Defining Arena. A sixth function of the neighborhood is that it often turns out to be a microcosm of the larger social problems confronting the society. Blight, pollution, and economic deprivation characterize current environment problems, but these are often recognized only at the neighborhood level. We have some evidence that individuals may rely heavily on the neighborhood as a base for reaction to social change or to organize themselves toward bringing about a change.

The question becomes one of whether the neighborhood is an appropriate unit or not. It is possible to see the neighborhood performing the function of differentiating problems that have an immediate character and a soluble base from those which are broader in character and are in the power of local neighborhoods to resolve.

Neighborhoods can provide programs for units of government and for other attempts at change which will be more effective in terms of planned social intervention. Also local neighborhoods, by providing the basis for cushioning the changes built into a mass industrial society, may permit people to respond to conditions of urban life more flexibly and effectively than formal organizations and welfare bureaucracies. At the same time, neighborhood organizations can play a major role in clarifying and defining solutions to urban problems by clearly differentiating among local problems that may be solved by local self-help and self-determination and those problems which clearly require wider bases and mobilization and collective action.

Where large-scale bureaucratic programs such as Model Cities and other efforts provide mobility for some members of the neighborhood but leave others relatively unaffected, the result has often discouraged many urban residents from engaging in a large-scale collective action. They feel their own interests are going to be lost or that the character of the local neighborhood will eventually be exploited by a small group. To the extent that working class and black ghetto neighborhoods have an abundance of local organizations, there exists the possibility for knitting such efforts together in order to project to larger, more centralized institutions, the needs of local areas. As such, the neighborhood serves as a kind of fulcrum for defining how individual energies are to be utilized in regard to a whole range of social problems.

In some cases, the individual will see the neighborhood as a fundamental way to focus on solutions. In other cases, it will become clear that no effective action can be taken through the local neighborhood. By providing these alternatives in strategies of change, local neighborhoods serve as a testing ground for devising optimal strategies in responding to different problems. As the priorities of government change from centralized to decentralized decision making, individuals are able to utilize their expertise and experience because they have already dealt with problems through a local neighborhood context.

Thus, protest actions which have occurred in local neighborhoods to get rid of sewage plants that were to be located nearby, or other efforts to resist or promote particular change efforts, serve as a crucial mechanism by which individuals are able to solve their problems.

Findings from the Detroit Study.   When we apply the notion of multiple functions of neighborhoods in the urban setting to our research in the Detroit area on black and white neighborhoods, some important findings emerge. When neighborhoods are ranked on the six major functions identified, we find that of the 16 black neighborhoods used in the study, 8 of them emerge as high or above the mean on the rankings. This is only true of 1 of the 12 white neighborhoods used. *Taken as a total measure of the functional role of neighborhoods, we found in our Detroit study that the local neighborhood was more likely to play a significant role in the lives of black individuals than in the lives of whites.*

In particular, we found that three functions of neighborhood were significantly higher among blacks as compared to white respondents. These included the function of neighborhood as a center of interpersonal influence; the neighborhood as a social context or reference group; and the neighborhood as an interaction arena (see Appendix, table 4A). There was no significantly greater likelihood that blacks used the local neighborhood as a center of mutual aid, as a status arena, or as an organizational base.

Creating a Typology of Local Neighborhoods

Our discussion of ways in which neighborhoods perform some important social functions in a mass urban society suggest that the degree of cohesion, the rate of interaction, and other separate measures provide only an abstract notion of the way in which neighborhoods are important. By putting together the various characteristics of social organization and orientation which individuals have to neighborhoods we have constructed a typology of urban neighborhoods which provides an important way to distinguish the rich variation of local communities in urban areas.

The first type of neighborhood that we have described is one which we have called an "integral" neighborhood. This is a setting in which there are close ties and frequent interaction between persons in the neighborhood. There is also a high degree of organizational life in the neighborhood. At the same time, the values and norms—the behavior patterns of the neighborhood—tend to be consistent with those of the larger society. For example, in political participation or in contacts with a governmental agency, persons in this neighborhood tend to rank high. This is a neighborhood, in other words, which has a local cohesiveness but at the same time has linkages with the outside world.

A second type of neighborhood that we can distinguish is one we have called a "parochial" neighborhood. This is a neighborhood in which individuals have a great deal of close interaction with one another but tend not to have linkages with the outside community. This may include areas such as public housing projects or other settings in which individuals, because of ethnic or other identifications, may have values and norms distinguished from those of the cultural majority. In this setting, the positive identification of residence tends to weaken somewhat loyalties to and participation in the larger community. What we are suggesting here is that the parochial neighborhood tends to be a self-isolating one.

A third type is the "diffuse" neighborhood, one in which there is a positive feeling toward the neighborhood, but interaction both at the formal and informal level is rather limited. People feel a great sense of common interest with their neighbors, but they engage in little collective action or extensive contact with their neighbors. This is a neighborhood frequently composed of people who may have moved to the area at the same time, who have a similar set of social backgrounds and characteristics and therefore do not need a great deal of interaction to share these common norms. The crucial factor in the diffuse neighborhood is the relative absence of turnover. If there is a great deal of in- or out-migration in this kind of setting, the fragile basis for neighborhood identification is seriously undermined.

Still another type of neighborhood is what Litwak and Fellin[21] have called the "stepping-stone" neighborhood. This is one in which the social institutions of the local neighborhood can quickly incorporate newcomers and where people who become active in the neighborhood do so because this is part of their required occupational role and fits in with their particular status-mobility plans. In other words, the individual who becomes active in the local PTA does so partly because his employer expects it, and also because his training as a member of such an organization will help his career and mobility plans. As he becomes more sophisticated in such activities he is liable to become more interested in moving on to "greener pastures." The local neighborhood often serves as one step in a planned mobility chain or ladder. The problems faced by the "stepping-stone" neighborhood include frequent turnover in leadership and consequently in effective planning. In such a neighborhood one's commitments lie less often in the local arena but are centered in other spheres of community and individual participation.

Yet another type of neighborhood is what we would call the "transitory" neighborhood. Residents in this neighborhood do not identify closely with the local setting and there is often a high degree of residential mobility. The norms of the neighborhood often suggest that one avoids participation in local entanglements either because the new families moving in tend to be different from oneself or because the very diversity of the neighborhood makes it difficult to feel any common set of values with one's neighbors. There may well be a degree of participation among neighbors in the form of a highly developed organizational life, but the pattern is liable to be very fractionated. There may be cliques that operate in the neighborhood, small groups who participate very highly and some of whom may claim to represent the total neighborhood. Such subgroupings tend to be separate from one another and to form pockets of activity which are not really knit together as a total pattern of neighborhood cohesion.

Finally, we can speak about what is frequently described in the literature on urban problems as the "anomic" neighborhood. This is one characterized by little identification of individuals with their local area and a minimum degree of either formal or informal social participation. This kind of neighborhood tends to have a high degree of estrangement from the values of any larger community and may be characterized by a low level of voting and political participation as well as indifference to ethnic, class, or social goals of the surrounding community. The anomic community is least likely to influence, mobilize, or alter its values through any form of socialization. The absence of social organization might in itself suggest an emergence of values which are likely to be deviant from those of surrounding communities. However, the more reasonable hypothesis is that residents of the anomic neighborhood engage in passive behavior, and although they display "alienation," they do so in a diffuse rather than in a specific way.

Detroit Study Findings. Findings from our Detroit study show that black and white neighborhoods tend to be different in terms of the types that we have been discussing. More black neighborhoods than white are classified as parochial or integral. A total of 8 of the 16 black neighborhoods have a high reference group orientation, either diffuse, parochial, or integral. This is true of only 4 of the 12 white neighborhoods studied (see Appendix, table 5A).

At the same time, we found that 1 out of 3 white neighborhoods tends to be of the stepping-stone variety. Only 3 of the 16 black neighborhoods fell into this category. One-quarter of the black neighborhoods were found to be anomic—exactly the same proportion as the white neighborhoods. Twice the number of black neighborhoods are either parochial or diffuse in character, compared to white neighborhoods. Consequently, *our findings strongly suggest that types of neighborhoods found in the black ghetto tend to be clustered somewhat differently than those found among neighborhoods within white population areas.*

We found another important factor that determined which type of neighborhood tended to be found more among the black sample— the extent of population turnover. This tended to be linked to whether they were classified as the cluster of positive reference neighborhoods (diffuse, parochial, or integral) compared with the negative reference oriented neighborhoods (stepping-stone, transitory, or anomic). Among the white sample, level of population turnover was no different, whether the neighborhood had positive or negative reference points. Thus, we seem to have identified that within the black community the pattern of neighborhood organization which emerges is strongly influenced by the degree of population turnover. The type of community found in white neighborhoods seems to be determined less by this factor.

Not only did we find differences in clusterings of neighborhood types in our sample of black versus white neighborhoods, but the importance for given functions of the neighborhood types was greater in the black community as opposed to the white community. For example, among black neighborhoods classified as transitory, there was an extremely low level of mutual aid. Those neighborhoods classified as diffuse, parochial, or integral had a relatively high level of mutual aid (see Appendix, table 6A).

In the use of various kinds of community services, black neighborhoods showed great variation depending on the particular type. Thus the stepping-stone and integral neighborhoods, along with the transitory, had a high use of community services. Diffuse, parochial and anomic neighborhoods were low. Variations between white neighborhoods were much smaller, although the integral neighborhoods had a relatively higher use of community services than did other types of white neighborhoods.

Thus we find from the research in Detroit that the way in which types of neighborhoods cluster is different in white and black population areas, but that the functions of local contexts differ as well. The neighborhood in the black ghetto results not only in different local community forms but their role is a more significant one for black individuals than it is for whites.

Neighborhood Heterogeneity as a Keystone of Black Ghetto Structure

Given the fact that we can identify different functions for neighborhoods and that we can group neighborhoods according to a series of different types, is there any way to talk about the dominant or basic force shaping neighborhoods? We believe that the factor which can be most readily used in this way is the diversity of socioeconomic levels within a given neighborhood.

This factor of neighborhood heterogeneity is a crucial one, partly because our conventional notions of group cohesion seem to require a high degree of homogeneity to work. It is this commonality of neighbors which appears to be the major factor in defining an area as a true neighborhood or not. Numerous studies have indicated the elements which need to be looked at in determining whether such commonality exists.

Robert Angell, in his classic study of the moral and social integration of cities,[22] concludes that homogeneity is the major determinant of social integration in American cities. Angell found that the greater the homogeneity of persons with respect to various statuses they hold, the greater the indices of social cohesion. A more recent analysis of neighborhoods tends to confirm this argument. Susan Keller concludes that it is the heterogeneity of populations which yields the impersonalized living assumed by urban theorists, and which at the same time disputes the role of the neighborhood.[23] Social participation, then, is seen as being focused outside the immediate neighborhood unless there is a high degree of commonality found within that area.

While agreeing with the bases for this argument, Fellin and Litwak argue that the problem of heterogeneity may not be so great as it appears:

This factor may be less valid today, owing to the development of mass communication in the enlargement of the middle class stratum in current society. The relevant question in regard to heterogeneity involves the extent to which value differences sometimes make communication between people difficult, differences may also serve complimentary needs and lead to cohesion. When values are contradictory, people are polarized along value positions, group cohesion is unlikely. However, extreme polarization of values is not common in our society.[24]

Our argument would be that in the black ghetto, this degree of polarization does in fact exist and that it is defined along the axis of local neighborhood. What characterizes the black ghetto is, in fact, the paradoxical fact that neighborhoods are often created on artificial bases to be either more or less heterogeneous than they would otherwise be.

In other words, the tendency is for neighborhoods in black ghettoes to be divided according to two extreme types: (1) a type of neighborhood in which there is a high degree of status difference among individuals living in that area; and (2) a neighborhood in which the common status positions of individuals are imposed through administrative policies involving public housing or ADC or other forms of aid.

It is our contention that this artificiality of neighborhood structure works against the process of black community cohesion. Thus in Suttles' discussion of neighborhoods he states that homogeneity in a neighborhood may be so great that it becomes oppressive:

In the long run, however, the most important consequence of project (public housing) living may be the way it restricts most opportunities to achieve a stake in the prospects of the local community and to develop the kind of leadership and social differentiation that is so critical in forming a stable, moral community.[25]

The very character of status similarity prevents the process, which Litwak and Fellin describe, developing healthy complementarity of interests in a neighborhood. *This suggests that the most viable form of local neighborhood organization is one in which there is a moderate degree of heterogeneity.*[26]

Let us review the path we have travelled. We have described the degree of heterogeneity which characterizes many black ghetto neighborhoods. We have indicated that the significance of heterogeneity is multiple in character. First of all, it tends to be associated with particular types of local neighborhoods—the transitory and the anomic types. These are neighborhoods which are very weak in terms of social organization and very ineffective bases for developing sources of individual and group solidarity. In addition, we have noted that the extent to which neighborhoods, regardless of type, tend to be high in hetero-geneity is greater in black ghettoes than it is in other types of com-munities (see Appendix, tables 8A–11A).

This means that the effects of social compression upon the total unit of the black ghetto structure are most sharply manifested at the local community level. This very frequently generates the type of situation in which there is status heterogeneity of a high order and, in turn this heterogeneity produces a type of neighborhood which forms a weak struc-ture for effective social and group action.

Policy Implications of Neighborhood Analysis

There are a number of significant lines of argument that follow from our findings both at the macro- and micro-levels of social action. We can see that the "Great Society" programs of the 1960s, built around the concept of maximum feasible participation at the local level, were poorly related to the nature of black ghetto structure. This concept was most prevalent in the Model Cities Program, which assumed that these areas lacked a high degree of community organization and therefore needed local participatory bodies such as elected boards or other groups in order to provide people with an effective voice in politics.

To the extent that black neighborhoods are heterogeneous in character, the development of representative citizen groups to serve on Model Cities' boards and in similar policy-making roles would be more difficult than in comparable white low-income homogeneous neighborhoods. Moreover, the existence of multiple status groups in a neighborhood, and the resulting degree of nonrepresentation that is liable to occur once a Model Cities board is selected is bound to be a serious problem.

The concept of Model Cities programming presumes fairly stan-dardized notions about the low-income or ghetto neighborhoods and its functions. It ignores the differences of local units that our analysis showed to be a major factor within the black ghetto. Does it follow then, from what we have observed, that programs which begin with the local neighborhood as the unit to be focused on will be more effective?

Our findings with regard to the black ghetto neighborhoods suggest that creating political power at the local neighborhood level has as many serious difficulties as developing policies which treat all neighborhoods in standardized ways. In other words, the concept of local control as defined by a participation in which residents of an area determine programs and policies of the institutions which affect them, can operate quite effectively as long as the degree of homogeneity within that neighborhood is sufficient to permit effective knitting together of groups in the area.

Where there is a situation of highly polarized neighborhood types within a community, the effectiveness of the local neighborhood as an organizational base becomes seriously undermined. On the one hand, the neighborhood which is high in heterogeneity may simply not serve as significant a role as a more homogeneous neighborhood in the lives of individuals. For example, when we examined the six major functions of neighborhood we found that both black and white heterogeneous areas were less often reference groups or centers of interaction than homogeneous locales. Among the black sample heterogeneous neighborhoods were less often organizational bases or centers of interpersonal influence. Thus the significance of the neighborhood, the kinds of roles it can play in the lives of individuals, is enhanced by a moderate degree of heterogeneity but is diminished by a high degree of heterogeneity.

Summary.   What we have introduced to our discussion in this chapter is the dominant role which, we argue, is played by the local residential neighborhood within the black ghetto. At the same time, the paradox we have identified is that the forces creating the ghetto itself mitigate against the local neighborhood's serving as an effective social unit. These shaping forces are focused within the black ghetto on those neighborhoods which take on an extremely homogeneous or heterogeneous character.

The resulting processes of local organization are therefore altered. Where a neighborhood is extremely diverse, in terms of the status composition of its residents, the forms of association which develop and the effectiveness of such forms are dependent upon the evolving of effective strategies at that local neighborhood level. The implication of having highly heterogeneous neighborhoods is that the strategies employed in moderately heterogeneous neighborhoods are simply not going to work. Among these is the strategy of having a relatively small group of individuals or organizations within a neighborhood serve as "representatives" of the residents of that area. To the extent that heterogeneity is present and the groups speaking on behalf of residents are not selected on the basis of the divergence of interests, we can predict that the outcome of participation will be to heighten the alienation of some members of that neighborhood. They will resist the efforts of the leadership group or they will withdraw from participation in any ongoing social action or social change effort.

It is therefore the local neighborhood in the black ghetto community which serves as the fulcrum on which major social policies often rest. The success or failure of such programs—whether introduced from external governmental agencies or emerging from within the ghetto community itself—is liable to be identical. Without decision makers who understand the special character of black ghetto neighborhoods, the potential for effective social policy efforts is greatly reduced.

The critical fact about the black ghetto as a whole is the diversity of neighborhood milieux. In particular we have stressed the nature of internal variability. The black ghetto may appear as a monolithic pattern from the outside, but is in fact characterized by an essential duality: local neighborhoods which are often more uniform than similar white areas or which are frequently more mixed in terms of social levels and life styles and therefore less uniform than white neighborhoods.

Chapter V

The Role of Voluntary Associations in the Black Ghetto

Membership in their own segregated associations does not help Negroes to success in the larger society. The situation must be seen as a pathological one: Negroes are active in associations because they are not allowed to be active in much of the other organized life of American society.

> Gunnar Myrdal,
> *An American Dilemma*
> (New York: Harper and Row, 1944), p. 952

WE NOW TURN to another major facet of community systems—the role of local organizations. While not unique to the urban scene, the proliferation and growth of various kinds of associations seems to be highly correlated with the increase in urban life. Their importance in the urban setting is attested to by the fact that such organizations have been regarded as powerful divisive forces as well as unitive ones in ghetto society. They have been viewed as a reinforcement of the segmental, depersonalized nature of urbanism and at the same time as the substitute for, or the supplement to, the solidarity of the traditional family or neighborhood. Voluntary associations have been viewed as vehicles for individual social mobility and also as a means of societal change. Still another perspective suggests that they serve as a mechanism for those in power to consolidate their positions and to maintain the status quo.

The fact that voluntary associations have grown and flourished does not imply that their membership is evenly distributed throughout the population. The bulk of empirical sociological research on voluntary associations has been directed to the study of membership and participation.[1] As a result of these studies we know that membership and participation rates tend to be lower for young adults and rise to a peak in the age group of the late thirties and early forties, generally to decline thereafter. Overall participation rates do not appear to differ markedly by sex, although males are more likely to be members in large cities and females in smaller cities.[2]

The evidence with regard to race differences is extremely contradictory. Data from more recent studies suggest that membership in voluntary associations is actually higher for nonwhites at the lower income levels and that active membership is generally higher for nonwhites at all socioeconomic levels.[3]

The Black Underparticipation Thesis

One widely held view of social participation among blacks is that there is a low level of involvement in contrast to whites. A number of studies present an almost anomic picture of black Americans in which they are viewed as having few organizational resources. Social scientists have argued that the primary cause for this underparticipation is the lower socioeconomic status of blacks. Other factors such as lesser age variations in the black population, general alienation and "civic apathy" have also been cited as causative forces. This view contends that blacks simply lack past organizational experience, verbal and social skills, or other personal qualities which are supposedly prerequisites to participation in voluntary associations.

Given this analysis of the underparticipation of blacks in community life, various programs have stressed the need to organize the unaffiliated, to develop "maximum feasible participation." The "organization of the unaffiliated" black is predicated upon the assumption that voluntary associations are important in reducing apathy, fostering individual and group problem-solving, and promoting social integration. Hence, much of the success of white ethnic Americans has been attributed in part to the proliferation of ethnic organizations.[4] It is argued by many that increased black organization will similarly lead to increased assimilation and integration into the larger society.

The Compensatory Overparticipation Thesis

The second approach to the issue of black organizational participation has evolved from the notion that blacks are, in fact, exaggerated Americans. This view was originally discussed by Gunnar Myrdal. This argument sees blacks, in their efforts to become mainstream Americans, as "overdoing it": emphasizing aspects of the larger society that are visible signs of acceptance and assimilation. The black middle class is seen as being especially guilty of this overparticipation. The holding of membership in a variety of clubs and civic organizations is

seen as a major determinant of one's position in the internal stratification system of the black community. From this view, organization
occurs within the black community because of its special capacity to
confer status, prestige and power.

For Myrdal, the exclusion of blacks from American society has
been compensated for by excessive affiliation with local, voluntary
associations of the black community. In his analysis, it was not
uncommon to find blacks who belonged to a great many voluntary
groups. He regarded this type of participation to be unproductive in
the sense that it tended to separate one black person from another.
Also, status groups resulting from this overparticipation were rigid and
thus a severe impediment to black assimilation. Thus Myrdal states:

> We regard the great number of Negro voluntary associations as a sign of social
> pathology . . . they accomplish so little in comparison to what their members
> set out to achieve by means of them. . . . The average sociable club has only
> one or two dozen members; there is an intense rivalry between clubs for status
> and an equally intense rivalry between members within any given club for office;
> the club is often short-lived; it seldom aids the individual to achieve success or
> raises the level of the "race"; it is time consuming and the activities undertaken
> are heavily formalized.[5]

Some recent sociological studies have given further credence to this
view of "pathological" overparticipation. Researchers have confirmed
Myrdal's contention that blacks are more likely to participate in
voluntary associations than whites, and in one study it was found that
this was true for "Negroes of all social class levels when compared to
their white counterparts, but it was especially true for lower-class
Negroes."[6]

The "compensatory overparticipation" thesis has also played a
role in the development of action strategy. Generally, social interventions based upon this analysis have called for the development of
racially integrated associations whose goal has been to foster better
relations between the races. The integration of civil rights groups of
the early 1960s is an example of organizations based on this thesis.

A second strategy based upon this theory of overparticipation has
been especially supported by the works on Frazier[7] and Hare[8]. It calls
for the total rejection of existing black organizations. These are to be
replaced by new organizations which do not differentiate among blacks
on the basis of class or prestige. This approach has constituted a major
thrust in efforts of black nationalists to organize communities.[9] Once
again, this approach rests upon the assumption that increased black

identity can replace social class and status characteristics as a major factor in promoting associational ties.

How can it be that both arguments, one suggesting a pathological form of community underparticipation and the other as pathological overparticipation are occurring simultaneously? Is there any validity to either argument or must we reject both of them?

Resolving the Contradictory Findings.   In an effort to understand the roots of the conflict between the underparticipation and overparticipation arguments, a number of recent studies have attempted to take into account those factors which have proven to be the best predictors of voluntary association involvement. This has been made necessary, in part, by the increased visibility of black organizations, which has seriously questioned the idea of underparticipation in the black community.

Virtually every study of social participation in the United States has shown that the individual's socioeconomic status is the one most important predictor of involvement. In other words, the higher the person's income, the more education he or she has, and the more prestigious the occupation, the greater the likelihood that the person will belong to many community organizations.

The first sophisticated effort to look at black versus white levels of participation for the *same* socioeconomic level was carried out by Orum in 1966. He found that lower-income blacks were more active participants in voluntary associations than whites in the same economic level. He also discovered that middle and upper class whites were more active in the organizations that they belonged to than were their black counterparts. In other words, social class differences were simply not important and were virtually obliterated in terms of knowing how active a person is in various community voluntary associations, at least within the black population. At the same time, Orum concluded that voluntary associations are a major focus in the lives of black Americans. He says that "associations are a means of collective membership for Negroes where they are a means of collecting membership for whites."[10]

Orum's thesis thus contradicts both the underparticipation argument as well as the pathological overparticipation argument.[11] In his view, black participation might be seen as compensatory in that it is a contemporary response against historical barriers to social opportunities. Yet, there is nothing pathological about this. Rather, it can be inferred from Orum's analysis, that whites are *more* socially compulsive in their leisure-focused affiliations than are blacks.

A replication of Orum's study by Marvin Olsen[12] supports this analysis. Olsen found that using data for Detroit from the 1940s and for Indianapolis in the 1960s, there was a tendency for black participation to show an increase. Olsen's study shows that those blacks who had high ethnic identity tended to show higher levels of association involvement than did other blacks. This led Olsen to modify the compensation argument, suggesting that members of ethnic minorities, whether based on race, religion, or nationality, may become active in social and political affairs because of social pressures exerted upon them within their ethnic community. Members of such an ethnic community are often more aware of their common bonds and hence are more socially cohesive than are whites. "As a consequence, their ethnic communities serve as a salient reference group for them. If the norms of this community stress social and political activism, these people will tend to exert pressure upon one another to conform to these norms by taking part in a variety of activities aimed at improving their common condition."[13]

Olsen concludes his discussion by arguing that "the ethnic community thesis" is a complementary "not contradictory explanation of the tendency for blacks to participate more actively than whites of comparable socioeconomic and age levels in many social and political activities."[14]

The Functions of Voluntary Associations

To contextualize the debate between the argument of compensatory overparticipation and underparticipation in the black ghetto, let us examine those functions which have been singled out as the unique roles that voluntary associations can play in the lives of individuals. These involve four distinct types of functions:

1. An integrative or socialization function that develops group goals, community or societal cohesion.
2. A prestige-conferring role which is an important part of determining individual career advancement, as well as indicating to people that they are on their way to becoming members of a group by participating in the organizations associated with that group or class.
3. A problem-solving role aimed at dealing with specific issues which affect individuals and their daily lives.

4. "Expressive" activities, dealing with recreation, tension-release, and various forms of sociability.[15]

Voluntary associations can have a multiple character in that they play all of these roles or they can focus on only one of these. But the clear implication is that organizations are vital, not only for the individual but also for a community in what might be seen as its need to adapt and survive.

It is also important to recognize that while sociologists have defined voluntary associations as having a formal pattern in which rules and procedures are set down and where the needs of groups may take on the character of a set of "bureaucratic requirements," the term "voluntary association" may cover a wide range of structures. These may vary all the way from a card club organized by a group of friends which begins to advertise its meetings, all the way to the professional society which sets up not only rigid requirements for participation but elects members to represent others, and which has a structure that is quite elaborate in terms of local, regional, and national offices.

The term "voluntary association" is one that should be treated very broadly indeed. Moreover, we should be very careful not to require that their purposes be always explicit and self-conscious. A good example of this arose during research the author was conducting relative to school-community relations. During an interview with an elementary school principal in a predominantly Southern white neighborhood, the topic of active white local groups was discussed. After giving some thought to a question about "community organization" the principal responded: "oh, no, these people aren't very political." In this instance "organization" meant specific formal goals and politically focused activities. When the question was rephrased to say: "do people around here seem to get together to do things?" the school principal immediately responded: "oh yes, there is the Southerners' Club." This is a group of people who meet in backyards and who often discuss various things going on in the community. The principal then recognized that his definition of a "political" group was a rather formalistic one because the Southerners' Club was indeed a "parapolitical" organization.[16] It did not have to be politically organized to deal with specific problems or with specific political activities. But it certainly represented a potential source of discussing problems, clarifying opinions, interpersonal influence and a whole array of expressions of community involvement basic to the nature of this particular Southern white community.

When we think about voluntary associations, we are talking about so diverse a range of groupings that it becomes rather unproductive to speculate about what are the "ultimate purposes" of the organization. The four functions of voluntary associations may occur simultaneously, or we may be able, as observers, to note over time that some of these functions seem to play a greater role than others.

Sociological research on voluntary associations suggests that before we can fully evaluate the significance of a level of participation in such groups, we have to look at several things. We have to know the functions that the group performs for the individual and for the society, something about the existing structure of that organization, and whether it is a very formal type of structure or a relatively informal one. We also have to know something about the stated or intended purposes of the organization, whether it has a single and constant goal, or if it has several goals, and whether it shows a tendency towards being successful in pursuing one kind of goal versus another. In other words, a comparison of the function or the role of voluntary associations in the black ghetto as opposed to other communities requires a much more detailed and closer examination than has been available from previous research on voluntary associations.

Findings from the Detroit Study. In the nearly 1700 personal interviews taken in the Detroit area, a significant picture emerges of the role of voluntary associations among black and white respondents. We asked people not only the extent of their participation in organizations, but a wide variety of questions about what they do in these groups, the kinds of motivations that led them to participate, and something about the view of how these organizations run.

Included in the list of such groups were neighborhood block clubs, PTAs, church groups, various forms of civic associations, professional organizations, social clubs, and even political and social action groups. We have the whole panorama of voluntary association groups as they exist among the Detroit sample of black and white individuals.

If we look at the rate of participation, that is, at those people who belong to at least one voluntary association, we find that there is virtually no difference in the pattern for whites and blacks. Among males, 75 percent of those interviewed belonged to at least one voluntary association. This was true of 79 percent of the white males. Among females, slightly under two-thirds, 65.8 percent of the black women and an identical proportion of white women, belonged to at least one voluntary association. In other words, our study dismisses one of the frequent myths about black and white participation in the sense that, once sex is accounted for, the participation levels, by race, do not differ.

If we look at different social class levels in the black and white sample, we can detect a major difference in the level of participation. When we take the factor of family income, we find that a higher proportion of blacks than whites, with an income of $15,000 or more, participate in at least one voluntary association. At the opposite end of the income spectrum, that is, those individuals in families with incomes under $4,000, we find that nearly 2 out 3 black individuals belong to at least one voluntary association, compared with slightly more than 1 out of 2 whites. The following pattern emerges with regard to income: at the extremes of the socioeconomic ladder, blacks participate more heavily than whites.

When we use education as our measure of status, we find that among blacks with a college degree there are only 2.8 percent who do not have at least one voluntary association membership, compared with 7.1 percent of whites. Among individuals who have not attended high school, 1 out of 3 blacks does not belong to any voluntary association, compared with slightly less than 1 out of 2 whites.

Taking the occupational indicator of status, we find that among unskilled workers there are fewer blacks than whites who belong to no organizations. There are more whites in managerial and proprietary (self-employed) jobs who have at least one associational membership as compared to blacks in the same line of work.[17]

Voluntary Associations in the Black Community: Heightened Significance. The Detroit data show not only that the participation range for blacks is greater than it is for whites, but even more importantly, the functions of voluntary associations seem to be multiplied in the black ghetto (see Appendix, table 12A). We asked individuals to tell us which of a variety of experiences their participation in organizations provided. The number of reported functions of organizations among the black respondents in the study was significantly higher than among whites.[18] Moreover, the kinds of functions performed by black organizations are of special interest to us.

For example, functions which have to do with "learning about how to improve my own economic condition," or "meeting people who have helped me improve my job or general economic situation," or "meeting people who are a better class of the community," were kinds of experiences that blacks reported significantly more often than whites as part of organizational participation.

The functions of "making new close friends," "learning about city government and the community," "coming in contact with new ideas and ways of thinking," or "giving me a chance to express my own skills and talents" were roughly equal in numbers of reported experiences for blacks and whites.

In other words, *the data from Detroit suggest that blacks rely very heavily on organizations and that black voluntary associations carry a special burden in terms of the social mobility of the individual.* Nor is this participation to be treated simply in terms of the more superficial status-striving among individuals. But rather it is linked to special knowledge about work careers and the patterns of community leadership. "Learning the system" in the ghetto is therefore a major task pursued through voluntary association participation.

To the extent that our Detroit data underscore the *multiplicity* of functions carried out by black organizations, we have support for the view that if there is an overparticipation by blacks in voluntary associations, it is for good reason. Individuals in the black ghetto are relying on their participation in voluntary associations not only for primary group contacts, friendships and associations with others, but also as a vehicle for learning the skills of social mobility as well as "cashing in" on those skills.

Thus, in direct parallel to the role of the local neighborhood, we have identified the voluntary association in the black ghetto as carrying a heavier than usual burden of community functions in comparison with the white community. Voluntary associations in the black ghetto contain a broader spectrum of individuals than do those in the white community. The combination of their multiple functions and the heterogeneity of their composition are distinguishing focal points for the role of voluntary associations in the black ghetto.

Status Conflict and Black Ghetto Organizations

If, as we have previously indicated, black ghetto social structure involves social compression in terms of the neighborhood setting, we may well ask the question: "does the multiplicity of functions performed by voluntary associations in the black ghetto also generate status conflict within these organizations?"

In order to respond to this question, we need to draw on a spe-

cial part of our overall research project, in which some 200 officers
or leading members of voluntary associations were given a special
interview about the group in which they were most active.[19] This
sample of some 200 local organizations serves as a basis for providing
us with insights about the character and structure of a wide variety of
voluntary associations in the black and white community. In the black
ghetto, the block clubs in particular provided us with much of the data
about the role of the local organizations (see Appendix, table 14A).
We inquired whether the differences in education between members
caused conflicts or whether group discussions revealed sources of
misperception, misunderstanding, or forms of dissensus in groups
that could be traced to the differences based on income, occupation,
education, or similar factors. In comparison with white organizations,
our Detroit research indicates there was a pattern of higher status
conflict issues in black organizations.

We may now explore in some detail the way in which black
organizations respond to the challenge of integrating within its membership persons of a wider variety of social statuses. In order to do
this, we must keep in mind the special character of the voluntary
association which is rather like that of a more intimate and usually
smaller primary group. Members have a great deal in common but
have organized a formal structure to develop their shared interests
and goals. We can broadly describe the modes by which voluntary
associations adapt to either neighborhood or membership heterogeneity (see table 1). These fall into three basic kinds of mechanisms:
selective recruitment, structural change, or goal shifting.

Enforced Homogeneity. The first of these, which we have called "selective recruitment," or "selective expulsion," involves the organization's
sifting and sorting of its membership. In this process, various status
characteristics of members become salient in terms of defining whether
the group can function in a cohesive manner. If individuals are very
different in terms of age, or social class, the possibilities for internal
conflict are increased. The organization reduces this by selectively
seeking out particular individuals with similar social status. In some
sense we might refer to this as a kind of elitism, in that it keeps the
membership fairly exclusive. In addition, selective recruitment serves
to limit the size of the organization, to attract members who have
similar characteristics, and to exclude those who do not conform to
the norms of the organization.

TABLE 1

**Modes of Voluntary Association Adaptation
to Neighborhood or Membership Heterogeneity**

1. Selective recruitment-expulsion	*2. Structural adaptation*	*3. Goal displacement*
(a) Elitism—keep small and be exclusive	(a) Give leadership different functions than in other situations. Centralize, select leader on special criteria	(a) Develop different goals for diverse interest groups in organization
(b) Select leaders or members based on similarity with others in group	(b) Formalize roles— rules, division of labor, etc.	(b) Frequently shift goals or innovate with different programs
(c) Ostracize deviant members	(c) Provide special formal mechanisms to handle conflict	(c) Emphasize goals that are integrative for the group rather than instrumental
	(d) Use informal power to deal with conflict	

These processes need not be formalized by rules or explicit statements of exclusivity. However, over time, an organization may be shown to have a membership with a homogeneous composition even though we know that the organization is capable of drawing upon a diverse population.

Structural Adaptations. A second means by which organizations may cope with heterogeneity involves the altering of its internal structure. This may take a variety of forms. One of these has to do with altering the way in which the leadership of the organization functions. For example, leaders may take on the special skills of knitting together a diverse membership. In this sense, the leadership may need to develop what social psychologists define as "social-emotional" or "integrative" skills.[20] These enable leaders to develop cohesion in the groups even though individual members of the organization may have many differences of opinion and outlook.

Often leadership itself becomes a basis for adaptation in terms of the types of personalities of the leaders and their "style of leadership." The question arises whether the leader should press for the accomplishment of specific tasks or whether he or she should stress the skills necessary for relating to the divergent members of the group? In the heterogeneous group the leader often must do both things effectively.

The structure of an organization may be related to its membership in terms of formalization. If the organization is extremely diverse in its membership, there may be a greater need to have special rules governing the behavior of members, election procedures, the division of labor within the organization, who shall take on special roles, etc. All of these aspects, which make the organization more formalistic, are required because the membership itself is so diverse that the usual informal means of communication and establishing of procedures are ineffective.

In addition, if an organization wants to relate to a heterogeneous membership, provision must be made for special ways to handle conflicts. This might be by subcommittees, negotiating groups, grievance committees, or any sort of mechanism which recognizes the possibility of internal conflict and the need for the organization to have built-in methods for dealing with it.

Finally, an organization which is diverse in character may recognize that no set of formal administrative or structural arrangements will deal fully with the special problems of that structure, and that the real need is to maintain a *flexibility* in structure in order to facilitate informal means of exercising power. In this sense, the organization may stress the need to have a lot of informal contact before meetings, a chance for people to relate to one another, to know how to modify what would otherwise be incompatible positions, and to insure in various ways that the anticipation of conflict may tend to reduce its disruptive influence on the organization.

Goal Displacement. There is a third process which has been elaborately discussed in various studies of larger- and smaller-scale bureaucracies. This is the process of "goal displacement." As social scientists have developed this concept, it means that any organization which starts out with a single goal, particularly one that is general in nature, is likely to find over a period of time that the focus will shift from the original goal. Thus, the large-scale welfare bureaucracy, which seeks to serve the needs of the poor, may find after some time that the basic need served is to create a new class of professional or high prestige occupational roles.[21]

The process of goal displacement means that the day-to-day operations of an organization, even a small voluntary association, are liable to produce a gradual shift in emphasis from the activities focused on at first. In the heterogeneous organization, goal displacement results in a stress on what we might call "instrumental activities", namely, the accomplishment of specific political and social goals. This is because so much time is spent with "expressive social goals"—keeping the group united. This distinction indicates that an organization, in order to function, often needs to provide a mixture of very specific activities along with those aspects of sociability and warm interaction necessary for any human group. This is particularly significant in the light of Myrdal's belief that participation in black organizations is focused on an emulation of white organizations.

Myrdal and others have suggested that black organizations put a great emphasis on the "expressive" or "integrative" goal activities of their organizations. Thus much of the personal motivation and satisfaction which people derive from these organizations is based not on what is accomplished for the individual in terms of a political or social gain, but on fellowship.

How do the ideas of goal displacement and "expressive goals" fit together? Our argument is that if organizations are extremely heterogeneous in character, even though they may have as their stated purpose a very specific utilitarian goal (for example, improving the job situation of blacks in a local community or providing social services) and even as they pursue that goal, the focus will center on keeping the group together.

The reason for this is that the context of black organizations is one in which neighborhood diversity is often commonplace. Secondly, as we noted in our Detroit sample, black organizations have a broadly based participation by high and low status individuals. It is not surprising, then, that black organizations adapt to these conditions of status diversity and heterogeneity by manifesting a high degree of goal displacement.

We now have a set of specific consequences which flow from ghetto social structure and its role on the impact of voluntary associations.

Neighborhood Setting and Black Voluntary Associations

We have discussed some conceptual and empirical patterns of voluntary associations in the black ghetto in relation to internal consensus under conditions of membership diversity. But what about the external setting —the heterogeneity of neighborhood populations? What is the evidence from the Detroit study which links neighborhood heterogeneity to voluntary association structures? How have these structures survived in spite of heterogeneity?

We find that in heterogeneous neighborhoods there are relatively smaller memberships in organizations than those found in homogeneous black neighborhoods. Among black areas about 1 in 5 of the organizations in heterogeneous neighborhoods have 100 or more members, compared with 3 in 10 for homogeneous settings. Among white neighborhoods we find that the vast majority of neighborhood organizations have 50 or more members. The heterogeneous white neighborhood has organizations which tend to be particularly large in size (see Appendix, table 15A).

With regard to membership turnover and the stability of size in the organization, the pattern of difference between heterogeneous and homogeneous neighborhoods is even more pronounced. Thus, only 1 in 3 of the organizations found in black heterogeneous areas shows a growing membership. This compares with more than half of those groups found in homogeneous black neighborhoods (see Appendix, table 16A). At the same time, about 2 in 5 of the black organizations in heterogeneous neighborhoods have stable memberships.

What about the leadership functions in a black organization? High "trust" is reported significantly more often between leaders and members in black organizations found in heterogeneous settings as opposed to those in homogeneous settings. In addition, when asked about the characteristics of the leader who was chosen, respondents in black heterogeneous neighborhoods mentioned far less often that leaders were chosen because they had good ideas and programs. More often, the views of the leadership "reflect the thinking of the majority of the group." Also more often, the leaders are chosen "because they have past experience in organizations" or "because of their education and social standing." The pattern of leadership selection also put a premium on conformity and past organizational experience but little emphasis on innovative ideas and programs (see Appendix, table 17A).

It is important to note that, although we find significant differences between black and white organizations in homogeneous versus heterogeneous neighborhoods with regard to leadership and selective recruitment, in terms of structure we find little difference. There seems to be no unique structural characteristic such as greater formalization (more use of rules or different levels of authority) or bureaucratization found in black organizations in heterogeneous versus homogeneous neighborhoods.

The Detroit research indicates that organizations in black homogeneous (versus heterogeneous) neighborhoods are reported by their officers to be willing more often to take on a special problem in the neighborhood, a problem not usually part of the organization's concerns. In contrast to the organizations in the heterogeneous black neighborhoods, groups in other settings tend to be innovative and open to new programs.

Is Organizational Survival Enough?   What is the effect of neighborhood setting on the goals the organization concerns itself with? When we asked people about the major stage of the group, the following "cohesion building" goals were listed: "trying to expand membership," "trying to build group spirit where it has been lacking," "developing a procedure for trying to get people of different backgrounds to work together," or "just developing a sense of its own identity." We found significantly more often that black organizations in homogeneous neighborhoods were preoccupied with these kinds of goals.

In contrast, "instrumental" goals, new programs, the need to clarify goals, "to move from one single goal to several goals," were the kinds of effort emphasized in black organizations found in heterogeneous neighborhoods. Moreover, when we asked people what were the more successful programs that their group had pursued in the past, far more often in the homogeneous neighborhood, the report was that some sort of expressive goal had been pursued. In other words, a membership drive, some development of group solidarity, or something of this kind was mentioned rather than the accomplishment of a specific goal such as bringing about a change in the behavior of a city agency or a local school.

What we have is a basic dichotomy. The organizations found in heterogeneous neighborhoods in effect insulate themselves from the social status diversity in their neighborhoods. Rather than confronting the problem of having to deal with a varied population, these organizations carefully screen out people who have different values and social backgrounds from their own membership. As a result, these groups are able to pursue important instrumental activities. They are not preoccupied with trying to maintain group consensus. They do not spend a large portion of their time debating the extent of commitment of people to the organization.

But this ability to act has a rather high price. In exchange for this capacity to act on specific goals, these organizations become unrepresentative of their neighborhood. Instead they represent those individuals in a given setting who share a great deal in common. These organizations are able to succeed with their stated goals but the question becomes "are these the goals of the neighborhood in which they are located?"

The black organization found in the homogeneous neighborhood has more than the expected share of internal conflict. Yet these kinds of organizations are remarkably innovative. The question is how successful are they? In the groups found in homogeneous black areas, there is a pronounced degree of goal displacement. That is, these groups because they open themselves up to large membership and do not selectively recruit, may be more diverse than the organizations in the black ghetto found in heterogeneous neighborhoods.[22] What we find in the black organization located in a homogeneous area is that there is a strong emphasis on expressive goals. These organizations expend almost more energy than seems necessary to maintain effective internal solidarity.

In some sense, then, the Detroit research reverses what we might ordinarily expect—that the source of status conflict is not found within the structure of voluntary associations in heterogeneous neighborhoods, but instead is expressed through the social distance or insulation between those organizations and their surrounding milieu. Black organizations in a setting that is diverse cope with the problem by avoiding it. In contrast, groups in homogeneous black neighborhoods appear to take on the unmet issues of representatives in organizations. They struggle with problems of internal consensus by modifying their organizational procedures, spend time on developing cohesion, and, in general, risk taking on problems that the groups in more heterogeneous areas neglect.

Correlates of High and Low Status Conflict in Black Organizations

The pattern that we find in Detroit suggests that those organizations in the black ghetto which have a great deal of status conflict built into them are usually organizations which do not selectively recruit their members. We have found that this process of selective recruitment occurs heavily in heterogeneous neighborhoods. Where it does not occur in such neighborhoods or when we are focusing on the homogeneous neighborhood, how is this internal conflict handled by the black organization in question?

Size

Our data show that the size of the groups in the black community with a high degree of status conflict is larger than that of groups with low status conflict.[23] By reducing the size of the organization and thereby maintaining a more "primary group" type structure, it is possible for persons of potentially diverse statuses to work together more effectively. Sociologists have argued about the optimal size of a primary group, but generally the notion of 30 or under is considered to be some sort of cutoff point. We find that better than 2 out of 5 black organizations with low status conflict have 25 or fewer members. This contrasts with about a quarter of the organizations with high status conflict.

In other words, those organizations within the black community which avoid internal status conflict are the smaller ones. If we look at white organizations, we find that no such relationship exists. For example, there are twice as many white organizations with smaller memberships that have high status conflict as have low. Thus, the whole set of dynamics appears to be quite different in white organizations.

Growth

Turn to another characteristic: membership turnover and size increase. Black organizations in which status conflict is high frequently reveals that they are expanding structures with new members outnumbering those leaving. At the same time, we find that black organizations low in status conflict are significantly more likely to have stable memberships. Similar patterns also prevail with regard to white organizations with high and low status conflict. What seems to distinguish the white organization with built-in status conflict from its black counterpart is that more often the white organization has a similar size but a turnover of membership, whereas the black organization is more likely to have an increase rather than a turnover in membership.

This is an extremely important point. It implies that as new individuals come into a black organization, the likelihood that status conflict will emerge is greater than in a white organization. What seems to cause status conflict in the white structure is not size itself but an instability in terms of membership.

Leadership

Let us now look at the leadership patterns found in high and low status conflict organizations. The Detroit research shows that in both black and white organizations with high status conflict, leadership is reported significantly more often not to have the same education, income, or occupation as the membership. This is especially pronounced in high status conflict black organizations. Leadership in these groups "takes a stand against the majority of the group" three times as often in high status as in low status groups.

Furthermore, leaders in high status conflict groups more often are praised for taking the role of expressive or "social emotional" leaders, that is, providing a lift to the people when they are feeling low. Less often are they praised for carefully following the rules of the group. The role of leadership in high status conflict organizations is pushed in the direction of having to stress the integrative functions of leadership—keeping the group together—instead of trying to push through specific programs and following rules.

In terms of the formal structure of organizations, we found important differences between high and low status conflict groups. In terms of having several levels of authority and having set procedures, we find the high status conflict organizations are higher on the indicators than the low status conflict organizations. This is true to some extent as well in the differences between high and low status conflict white groups.

Another difference is that the leadership role in the high status conflict black organizations has to be flexible and not take the same approach to different problems. This willingness to act differently "depending on what the situation calls for" is significantly more likely in high status conflict black organizations than it is in any other type of voluntary association found in the survey. At the same time, we find that the white high status conflict organization more often has more offices and committees in its structure.

Process

In addition, the high status conflict black organizations have to set up or use special committees in dealing with various problems. This involves a series of structural modifications which take place in order to handle the internal heterogeneity of their membership. Besides the formal structural modifications, organizations in the white and black communities which have high status conflict, report much more often a "lot of conversation before and after meetings." Thus, the "greasing of the wheels of interaction" requires that there be contact beyond the formalities of participation in the structure. Without this additional informal and flexible exchange it is more difficult for these organizations to function.

What about the process of group consensus in high status conflict organizations? Our evidence here is both consistent and striking. In high status conflict groups there is less often agreement on basic goals. Three times as often in high status conflict organizations black respondents report that there is "substantial lack of agreement about goals."

We also find that the black organization with internal status conflict has the highest level of complaint with regard to distractions and irrelevant content during group meetings.[24] For example, we find that more often in the black high status conflict organization the complaint that "when people disagree at meetings, they usually do so for other than good reasons." Moreover about three times as often as in the low status conflict, black groups' interviewees from high conflict black groups indicated that people were "doing their own thing versus working on the problem at hand." Four times as often in the high status conflict black group it is said that "the organization is trying to handle too many different issues." The same proportion of difference occurs in regard to the organization "spending too much time keeping people in agreement than in going ahead with the meeting's programs."

Similar tendencies occur in white organizations but only in regard to the issue of people not participating at meetings in terms of useful content, or the feeling that the organization is trying to handle too many problems.

Innovation

What about the issue of innovation in the high status conflict organization? High status conflict groups, as much as low status conflict groups, report willingness to take on innovative programs or special problems. However, among white organizations the low status conflict group seems to be highly conservative in character, being far less willing to take on new programs but at the same time more willing to take on special problems. They demonstrate a capacity to respond rather than a conscious effort to continue to innovate. This is an important implication about the white organization being less significant as a vehicle for responding to social change than organizations in the black community.

What about the question of goal displacement? We find that when black respondents talk about the goals of their organization in the high status conflict group, there is a significantly greater emphasis on integrative goals such as trying to build the identity of the group, trying to build group spirit or trying to get people of different backgrounds to work together. Similar patterns are found between the low and high status conflict white groups.

Effectiveness

Some important differences are emphasized in black groups in regard to the kinds of goals pursued successfully or which are projected into the future. While all respondents tend to report that their groups are working on or have been successful at very instrumental goals, such as changing city policies about street lighting or changing school curriculum; when we look at the high status conflict black organization it is distinct because of the greater frequency with which it talks about successful goals in expressive terms, that is, building spirit, developing a feeling of cohesion, rather than the accomplishment of specific goals.

In terms of new programs contemplated, there is a similar trend. The black high status conflict organization is more expressive in character. At the same time, we find that the low status conflict group looks rather similar. Once again, we have an indication that white organizations which avoid status conflict are groups engaged in rather innocuous kinds of activities and do not require movement toward specific goals or activities.

Summarizing Adaptation Processes to Status Conflict. Our research in Detroit has confirmed the notion that under conditions of either internal diversity in an organization or the existence of neighborhood diversity, there seem to be unique organizational responses that emerge from our sample of voluntary associations. We found that the scope of voluntary associations in terms of membership, as well as the very important functions performed by such structures, made them unique elements of community organization.

Given their special importance in the black ghetto, the special problem confronted by black organizations, how to build in a diverse membership or how to function in a setting which is diverse, is a major focus of community process. We defined a set of mechanisms that organizations use when they are confronted with problems of heterogeneity. The voluntary association tends to develop, even under the best of circumstances, into an oligarchy of the most active members. Such organizations can manifest these patterns and be expressive of "grass roots" democracy if those who are not involved are somehow represented by the active minority. Neighborhood heterogeneity tends to call into question this "workable" relationship.

Once we have characterized a constituency as a local neighborhood and we know that it tends to have a great deal of diversity built into it, the question of how an organization relates to that constituency becomes a matter of modifying its structure, modifying its goals or redefining who its constituents are. In our Detroit study there was a distinct pattern among organizations found in the heterogeneous black neighborhoods. The organizations located in such settings were remarkably homogeneous. They tended to develop this pattern in response to what we have termed "selective recruitment," or the potentiality of selective expulsion. We did not directly identify how these processes work, but the patterns that we noted strongly suggested that selective recruitment made it possible for an organization to seem to have a great deal of similarity between its leadership and its constituency and yet be in a status diverse area.

Our findings are especially important because the organizations which we sampled among our black respondents tended, even more often than in the case of white organizations, to be of two kinds: local block clubs or local PTAs. Consequently, the very fact that these are neighborhood-based organizations and that they tended to have a great deal of status similarity among their membership, implies that they must exclude a number of individuals who live in that local setting. Thus, while these organizations seem to be successful as reported by their key officers and others, that very success is gained at the price of unrepresentation. This of course has been one of the major hypotheses with which we began this study. We have suggested that the status diversity of neighborhoods involves a process in which organizations and activities of local neighborhoods tend to be simultaneously intensified and crippled.

The successful organization located in a black heterogeneous neighborhood tends to be an organization which has been forced to be selective. At the same time, we find that in the homogeneous neighborhood, black organizations tended to be fairly high in innovativeness, open in membership, larger, and more expansive in character.

Yet these same organizations seem to pay the price of building in a fairly high degree of internal diversity. We found in the Detroit study that where organizations, whether located in heterogeneous or homogeneous neighborhoods, had a high level of status conflict built into them, their capacity to survive and adapt required some form of structural modification.

Those organizations within the black community which were experiencing a high degree of status conflict tended to modify their structure by becoming more likely to have a certain type of leadership, a type of leadership involving the skill of keeping people together even if this must happen at the price of moving ahead on specific goals. At the same time we find that the organization faced with status conflict often has to modify its formal structure to allow for more levels of authority and a longer hierarchy of decision-making; more committees or more different offices in the organization. This permits diverse status groups to have a voice.

The price of increasing the complexity of the formal structure is to reduce the flexibility and innovativeness of the organization. But the problem of the black organization of status diversity is not so much in the area of innovation but in the area of efficiency. Thus the complaints about people using the organization to "do their own thing." In these groups rapid and effective response to problems gives way to the maintenance of internal cohesion. In other words, the very survival of the group becomes an end in itself. Its capacity to persist under conditions of status conflict and diversity is of course a clear measure of its success.

The existence of black voluntary associations, given the problems of status diversity, may seem as nothing less than an exercise in futility. The special urgency for such groups to be effective is clearly underlined throughout our research. That is, often individuals use their organizational memberships for a wider variety of purposes. And often these purposes have to do with individual mobility and learning the skills of how to beat the system. Therefore, if we use as a measure the efficiency of an organization in decision-making and in reaching its goals, we will have overlooked the significant role of these structures in making up for the restricted access blacks have toward other kinds of structures in the society which provide individuals with channels of mobility and means for individual advancement.

The black voluntary association, then, can be seen as heavily burdened with the need to fulfill both community goals as well as individual ones. We found in our study that white organizations, particularly those that lacked status conflict, were often, in a sense, "coasting." They focused on expressive goals and did not seem to be in the position to innovate nor had they begun programs in recent years to the same degree that whites in high status conflict organizations appeared to have done.

For white organizations, the source of status conflict seemed to be the turnover of the membership in the organization, the larger size of such organizations and the tendency for such groups to be found in more heterogeneous neighborhoods.

We can review our findings in Detroit in terms of the following major differences between organizations in the black community and in the white community, and those located in homogeneous and heterogeneous neighborhoods:

1. Black organizations in heterogeneous neighborhoods utilize selective recruitment of members so that they have small memberships and show a slightly greater emphasis on integrative versus expressive goals.

2. Organizations located in black homogeneous settings place little emphasis on selective recruitment, and have organizational structures which show a mixture of bureaucratic qualities.

3. Black organizations in homogeneous neighborhoods show a high degree of goal displacement in the direction of innovative programs but of an expressive character.

4. Organizations in white heterogeneous neighborhoods are relatively open structures which rely heavily on modification of their internal functioning to reflect a highly centralized structure, but one which places an emphasis on a human relations rather than a bureaucratic approach. Goal displacement trends are evident but suggest the maintenance of a high degree of concern with instrumental rather than expressive goals.

5. Organizations in white homogeneous neighborhoods have hierarchical structures which closely fit the traditional model of a formal bureaucracy. Both a shift toward expressive goals and a continuing emphasis on instrumental activities characterize such groups. There is little innovative content to either type of goal.

6. Black organizations with a low degree of internal status diversity are more often found in heterogeneous neighborhoods than in homogeneous ones. The reverse is true for white organizations.

7. Black organizations with low status conflict are characterized by extensive use of membership screening, limited size, flexibility of structure, and a relatively high emphasis on instrumental as opposed to expressive goals.

8. Black organizations with high status conflict tend to show an extensive amount of goal displacement in the direction of expressive activities. They employ little selective recruitment or structural adaptation and place a relatively high emphasis on innovative programs.

9. White organizations with high status conflict use informal and flexible structural arrangements to stress instrumental goals and not to screen new members.

10. White organizations with low status conflict have a high degree of selectivity of membership and maintain a balance of activities between expressive and instrumental goals. They are also characterized by a low degree of innovation and a more limited range of goals.

Strategic Implications of the Survey Findings. Putting together these patterns we see that there is a very significant correlation between the neighborhood setting and the way in which a voluntary association operates. We have found that there are patterns of adaptation which appear in the black community in response to both internal and external sources of status heterogeneity. To the extent that black organizations in the heterogeneous neighborhood setting are successful, it is precisely because they do not reflect their surroundings. The potentiality for a high degree of clique formation is suggested.

This implies that there are a series of organizations operating side by side in black heterogeneous neighborhoods, each drawing from the separate constituencies contained within a common field of potential members. At the same time, the tendency for status conflict to be found in many organizations in black homogeneous neighborhoods suggests that these structures are drawing upon the maximum diversity in their neighborhood and possibly beyond. Both patterns imply that the relationship between what goes on in the voluntary association and what goes on in the neighborhood are intimately linked.

We began this chapter with some overall perspectives about the extent of participation in the black community. We have emerged from our analysis with the view that there seems to be qualified support for the argument that, if indeed voluntary associations represent a particularly intensive form of community life in the black ghetto, this very quality of involvement is enhanced by the heterogeneity found within many black organizations. The problems posed by this sort of diversity are responded to in a number of ways. A requirement of effective response is especially noted in our findings in Detroit. In this sense, the black voluntary association cannot emulate its white counterpart. Therefore, the argument that in fact black joining of organizations is nothing but the emulation of white structures is not supported in our findings.

What we find is that black voluntary associations take on a special character entirely their own. The search for solutions to community problems through voluntary associations must be seen as both challenging and frustrating. On the one hand, the voluntary association in the black community does not work in the smooth or automatic fashion that such organizations may operate in white communities when they are called upon to deal with specific problems. At the same time, it is clear that in the black ghetto, the voluntary association has a potential for implementing social change not generally found among counterpart organizations within the white community. As vehicles of social innovation and change, however, black voluntary associations must face the challenge of how to cope with or how to invent adaptations to the special dilemmas which they face. There is a challenge confronting voluntary associations which seek to function within a status diverse milieu. They must somehow either modify their structure, increase the homogeneity of their members, or evolve goals which preserve the ongoing structure of the organization.

If these adaptation mechanisms do not effectively function, the organization is likely to collapse. As we look at our Detroit data, we are examing those organizations which represent "the survival of the fittest." The structures that are still in existence have had to manifest successful coping strategies in the problems of status heterogeneity. Given the character of the voluntary association as a type of formal organization which stresses participation in decision-making within a context of a relatively homogeneous membership, this form of organization will have to be "stretched" in order to accommodate itself to the special conditions of its neighborhood and membership heterogeneity. But even if such organizations are able to survive and become effective in terms of their constituency, a further difficulty is presented relating to other organizations in the ghetto community.

The Linkage Function of Local Associations.   If in fact many groups find they must isolate themselves from some people who live in the local neighborhood, then what is the implication of their seeking to join with other groups beyond the local neighborhood? This presents the organizational structure which emerges in the black ghetto with a dual problem: devising mechanisms for existing in a locally complex setting and at the same time being in a position to manifest unity under the rubric of ghetto differentiation (see Appendix, tables 19A and 20A).

The implication is clear: to the extent that voluntary associations in the black community do not encompass even their own local neighborhoods, the possibility for living together and forming a pyramid of local groups to create a tight neighborhood cohesion is extremely limited. Even if it is granted that neighborhood organization is a crucial matrix within which to build community cohesion, the critical mass represented by a unit even as small as the elementary school district may be too extensive to be "represented" by black voluntary associations.

The building blocks of community which use neighborhood do not correspond with the patterns that are characteristic of black voluntary associations, especially as they are found in heterogeneous areas. As a result, if we wish to make a case for the role of building community from the neighborhood level up, we must take into account the extent of status diversity found in that neighborhood.

As long as black neighborhoods are homogeneous in character, then it is possible for black organizations to use effectively the base of the local geographical area. The energy and individual commitment that may go into the effort to devise strategies for local neighborhood survival of an organization may foreclose the possibility for developing linkages with other groups beyond the neighborhood. Therefore, even if success is gained at the local level, the range of problems which affect ghetto life are so frequently a matter of larger social forces than the local neighborhood, that the very success of such a local voluntary association may serve only as the most balkanizing of consequences.

A calculus of caution must go into weighing the alternatives of trying to build organizations at the local neighborhood level, given the character of ghetto social compression. If the choice is success at the neighborhood level versus the opportunity to move into wider social circles for the individual, the issue may be all too frequently clear: abandonment of the local neighborhood in terms of primary involvement and the seeking out of shared status value and social goals which may reflect views and behaviors divergent from those of one's neighbors and residential peers.

For the black ghetto itself, the question becomes one of attempting to utilize the existing local structures or of bypassing them in an effort to move effectively with regard to the important social goals of the community. Therefore, the call for maximum feasible participation may turn out to be one of the most dysfunctional pursuits for black ghetto residents. For the multiplication of organizations or the attempt to work through existing structures may prove a distracting and debilitating process whose results may prove meager indeed.

Only when participation at the local level means effective linkage with other structures can the task be justified. It is toward these linkages that our attention now turns as we pursue additional analyses from our Detroit findings, and the full description of the model of black ghetto structure that we have been developing.

Chapter VI

Leadership Structures in the Black Ghetto

For in all America it is assumed that every group contains leaders who control the attitudes of the group. . . . The leaders are organized locally . . . and they are conscious of their role.

> Gunnar Myrdal
> *An American Dilemma*
> (New York: Harper and Row, 1944), p. 712

This process of co-optation and a subsequent widening of the gap between the black elites and the masses is common under colonial rule . . . black people with certain technical and administrative skills who could provide leadership roles in the black communities but do not because they have become beholden to the white power structure.

> Stokely Carmichael and
> Charles Hamilton
> *Black Power: The Politics of Liberation in America*
> (New York: Random House), p. 13

UP TO THIS POINT in our discussion we have focused on neighborhood characteristics and organizational patterns in the black ghetto. It remains for us to pull these separate concerns together and to describe the mechanisms which make possible coherent and meaningful bases of community. Such functions devolve upon those persons most active in the black ghetto. In particular our interest goes beyond leaders of the "visible" and organizationally defined groups found in our Detroit study.

By reviewing the findings of that research we are able to describe the most important elements which link *static* patterns of community structure to what we might call the *dynamics* of leadership. This involves the role of individuals whose positions in organization or whose links with one type of organization provide the social glue by which communities function. It is in terms of this interlocking process that we may discuss what is unique about the black ghetto and what is reflective of the general role of local informal leaders and those who head up and play basic roles in the myriad of voluntary associations.

Informal Neighborhood Leadership:
The Role of the Reputational Activist

In defining the nature of leadership, political scientists have used at various times three basic approaches. The first of these has been to ask individuals in a particular population to name the persons who play important roles in making decisions. A second approach is to look at the various organizations and institutions within a group and to identify those persons with formal positions at the head of such organizations. A third approach is to trace out particular issues that are important to a community and look at the individuals who play a role in the process of arriving at a decision.

A somewhat classic instance of the first of these approaches can be found in Floyd Hunter's *Community Power Structure*.[1] Hunter relies on what is usually described as the "reputational" approach to power. In pursuing this orientation in the 28 neighborhoods in our Detroit study, we sought to identify those persons whose respect and reputation were visible enough so that they would belong in what could be called local leadership stratum within the community. We therefore asked the respondents, "is there someone around here who is an active person if you want to get something done?" In this way, for each of the neighborhoods where we had a cross-section of the people we interviewed, in both black and white areas, we were able to draw up a list of persons who were mentioned as "activists."

We then went to these individuals and gave them the same interview that we had given to other persons in our study. By this means, we created what is commonly known as a "snowball" sample, that is, we added the individuals into our analysis who were defined by others as playing important roles in the local neighborhood.[2]

Our concern was with that stratum or definition of leadership that is closest to what might be termed the "grass roots" level of the community. This involves individuals who are not visible externally, beyond the local arena and who are not necessarily officers or members of important organizations, but whose reputation for getting things done is recognized by their peers and their neighbors.

Types of Activists.   Compared with the average respondents we interviewed in our study, the activist in the black community tended more often to be male. In the white community there was no particular difference. When we looked at the age factor, we found that the activist in the black community is usually a person over the age of 50. In white neighborhoods we found exactly the reverse to the case. The activist was more often a younger person, more likely to be between the ages of 30 and 50. The typical respondent for our study in white neighborhoods was older than that age range.

In black communities the persons who were identified as "reputational activists," if they were males, were more likely to be in the age group under 30, and if they were female, were more likely to be in the age group of 50 and over. Within the white sample, this pattern did not prevail. Whether male or female, activists tended to be distributed in about the same way according to age as nonactivists.

In the black community the majority of neighborhood activists had incomes of under $10,000. While this was true of the black population in general, the fact is that the neighborhood activist seemed to have a similar income profile to all black respondents. In comparison, in the white sample, neighborhood activists tended to have generally an income of more than $10,000 which represented a higher mean income than the average white respondent interviewed. In terms of educational level, we found that the black neighborhood activist had an average distribution of education in comparison with other blacks interviewed. By contrast, a larger proportion of the white activist sample had a higher educational level than the majority of other white respondents.

In terms of occupational level, we found that black neighborhood activists were more likely to be in white-collar occupation than were other black respondents and that, in particular, there was a very large number of such persons who were in managerial and proprietary roles. In other words, they were often small businessmen who ran local stores and lived in close proximity to their place of work. This pattern fails to appear in the white community, where activists were often at the professional level but they were even more often in skilled and blue-collar occupations.

Relationship between Neighborhood Characteristics and the Role of the Activist. When we compare the heterogeneity of neighborhoods, we find a major difference appears in how many neighborhood activists are to be found. In both black and white heterogeneous neighborhoods, there are simply *fewer* neighborhood activists. At the same time, major differences between black and white heterogeneous neighborhoods still appear. There are more activists in black than in white heterogeneous neighborhoods.

Even more important than the existence of those activists is the extent to which persons in the neighborhood were aware of such individuals and could name them. In homogeneous white areas, nearly 1 out of 2 persons knew of someone who performed the role of an activist. This compared with only 3 out of 10 blacks living in heterogeneous neighborhoods. In other words, we find that not only are there fewer neighborhood activists in heterogeneous neighborhoods, but also that the number of persons who know of an activist is lower in such settings.

A majority of persons in white suburban neighborhoods were able to mention an activist. By contrast, black suburban neighborhoods were significantly low in terms of individuals knowing neighborhood activists. The neighborhood least likely to have individuals being aware of a neighborhood activist is the suburban homogeneous black area. We also found that suburban neighborhoods which were white had the highest levels of awareness of neighborhood activists (see Appendix, table 21A).

Tight-knit versus Loose-knit Patterns of Informal Leadership.   We have pointed out the differences in neighborhoods in terms of whether many people living there can name a local person who is "able to get things done." In this way, a layer of community leaders is identified and can be added to our understanding of the social structure. But there are additional insights about the role of these individuals that we need. For example it is important to note whether *among themselves* these neighbors are describing the same leaders. In other words, to what extent are the neighborhood activists a group of disparate individuals or a small and identifiable cluster?

The patterns of interlock between neighborhood activists is a measure of what we may term the "informal web." The density of this network is important to describe. But to establish that "informal" leaders exist in neighborhoods we need to know how many times the same person is named by other neighbors. Our Detroit research permitted such a comparison.

When we make such a comparison between black and white neighborhoods, we find the following: in homogeneous neighborhoods, regardless of race, it is more often the case that there are multiple nominations of the same activist than when the neighborhood is heterogeneous. At the same time, if we look at the differences within the heterogeneous neighborhood we find that more often the black heterogeneous neighborhood has multiple nominations of the same activist (see Appendix, table 22A). Two major points emerge from our

Detroit data: (1) The informal reputational neighborhood leader, a person whose opinions are often relied on by others, or who is felt to be able to get something done, is in a majority of cases a person known to several others. (2) Interconnection between neighborhood activists is more often found in the homogeneous residential area regardless of whether it is black or white.

The role that neighborhood homogeneity plays in the character of an informal leadership web is not difficult to surmise. Given the greater similarity of status, it is easier for individuals to seek out others for advice and counsel on personal or community matters. Asking people about candidates for mayor or the best laundry detergent are, from the standpoint of neighborhood communication, rather similar processes. Consequently, if the neighborhood is heterogeneous, its residents may find fewer neighbors on whom they can rely for information or skill to deal with local problems. Neighborhood social structure therefore delimits the capacity of informal leadership to function.

The "loose" character of the network of neighborhood activists has special significance for the black heterogeneous neighborhood. This type of setting faces a range of problems in terms of formal organizations and the role of voluntary associations. When we turn to the roles of the informal neighborhood activist, we seem to have a compensatory form of leadership: a person who doesn't necessarily belong to any organization but whose reputation for being able to have influence and to get things done is wide and diffused among many neighbors. At least we can say that this phenomenon of a "grass roots" form of leadership seems to be a significant element of the black heterogeneous neighborhood. The same phenomenon is developed in the white homogeneous neighborhood.[3]

We can take our analysis one step further by asking not only whether the reputation of any single neighborhood activist is diffused widely among the persons living in that area, but whether one activist knows another activist? Here we find a very important pattern in our Detroit data. For both blacks and whites, there is a tendency in homogeneous neighborhoods for activists to know each other—they can name each other when talking about persons who are active. At the same time, we find that the pattern of one activist naming another activist, the awareness of mutual power and influence, is least likely to occur in heterogeneous black neighborhoods (see Appendix, table 23A).

In black heterogeneous neighborhoods there is a modest level of "coherence" to the informal web of leadership. Some are named as activists by more than one person in the neighborhood but such persons are rarer than in homogeneous neighborhoods. In comparison to white heterogeneous areas, however, more activists get multiple mention. We also found that such informal leaders are not very likely to know each other. What happens if we put these two facts together? The picture which emerges in the black heterogeneous neighborhood is one of a "clique" structure. Activists appear to have a constituency among a small group neighbors but one leadership subgroup appears to be isolated from the next. Each informal leader has a kind of independent following—a kind of fiefdom in the midst of a diverse neighborhood milieu. The interlock which is less likely to be present among neighborhood activists in the black heterogeneous neighborhood describes an important dissipating characteristic of the informal power that we have identified with a particular stratum of the black and white neighborhood sample. The looseness of this informal web in black heterogeneous neighborhoods provides a further index of the extent to which heterogeneity, as a source of weakened neighborhood capacity to act, is most critical in terms of the black ghetto social structure.

The Voluntary Association Officer:
An Example of a More Formalized Community Leadership

A second form of a community leadership structure involves those persons who hold offices and important positions in the various voluntary associations. Our data permit us to discuss what kinds of people become active in organizations and play a major role in the voluntary association dynamics of the black and white communities.

In the sample of persons who belonged to organizations and held a formal position in such groups, we find that 52 percent in the black segment and 42 percent in the white group were women. The fact that somewhat more than half of formal leadership roles in black organizations are held by women cannot be attributed to chance.[4] We have already noted the preponderant number of males in the roles of neighborhood informal leaders in the black sample.

Among officers in white voluntary associations, more were in the age group 30–49 than were neighborhood activists or other members or nonmembers of groups. In the case of the black interviewees, fewer were in the age group over 50 than either neighborhood activists or other blacks in the sample. The result is that the age distribution of black and white organizational leaders looks almost identical: about half over age 50, two-fifths in the age range 30–49, and about one-tenth under age 30. There is no "generation gap" that characterizes black ghetto association leaders—at least vis-à-vis the white sample in our study.

Is there any evidence from our Detroit study that suggests the extent to which leadership of formal black organizations may be more elitist than in the white community? In other words, are the leaders of black organizations more likely to be cut off from their local neighborhood than are whites?

Using a range of measures we find that this does not seem to be true. For example, when we asked the question, "do officers of associations see a great deal of consensus between themselves and their neighbors," there is agreement to this view just as often among white as among black voluntary association officers. In terms of identifying neighborhood problems, we find that officers in black organizations are as likely as other blacks to describe a range of neighborhood problems and three times as likely to be aware of such issues as are white organization officers.

Within the black community, persons who are officers of voluntary associations have higher incomes, educational level, and occupational positions than the cross-section of the black sample. This same pattern prevails in the white sample. However, there is an important difference which we noted in our Detroit data: whites who are officers of voluntary associations, are relatively more concentrated in the higher income, occupational, and educational statuses compared to their race peers than among blacks.

In general, officers of voluntary associations are of higher status than persons who are not officers. At the same time, the extent to which the black community has a wider range of persons who are in the role of organizational officers distinguishes this pattern of leadership from that found in the white sample. In other words, the pattern of joining which, as we noted in chapter 5, seems to cut across social classes more widely in terms of black ghettoes, is also reflected in the pattern of leadership in organizations. The potential for drawing upon a wider range of individuals or using more fully the resources of the community is reflected in the "officer cadre" of black organizations.

Local Allegiance of Association Officers.   One of the arguments frequently raised with regard to the role of formal organizational leaders is that they are often distant from the local setting in which they function and that, to some extent, they are separated from the rank and file not only of their own organizations but also of their neighbors and friends. This charge has particular significance in the black ghetto. Not only is this a frequent criticism of the organizational leader in the black community, but our evidence from the earlier analysis suggests that where such status conflict exists within black organizations, it is a greater problem than within white organizations.

In terms of relying on neighbors' opinions, black officers of voluntary associations are as likely as whites to indicate such reliance. When we look at the extent to which friendship patterns of association officers are located in the neighborhood, we find that a majority of such officers among blacks indicate that most of their friendship contacts come from within their local neighborhood. This is significantly more often than in the case for whites. In other words, the officer of a black voluntary association is more likely to say that his close friendships or primary group ties are exclusively located in the neighborhood and is less likely to find such ties outside of the neighborhood. At the same time, however, these same officers of black voluntary associations are *less* likely to have their own status position fit that of their local neighborhood than is the case for activists.[5]

When examining the informal neighborhood activist we raised the question of the role that the multiple nominations played: did one neighborhood activist know of another neighborhood activist? We can ask the same question with regard to association officers. Here we find that regardless of neighborhood setting it is more likely that a respondent who is an officer in a voluntary association also knows of another officer of a voluntary association. The interlink between one formal leadership role and another is closer in all white neighborhoods compared to all black neighborhoods.

When we look at the heterogeneous neighborhood we find that there is a general decline in the extent to which officers in one organization know officers in another. We can summarize this difference by stating that if we take the neighborhood in which there is likely to be the lowest overlap in formal leadership patterns, it will be the black heterogeneous neighborhood. The contrast is sharpest with the homogeneous white area, which is most likely to be a setting in which one officer in a voluntary association knows about an officer in a different organization.

The Overlap Between Formal and Informal Leadership

We now come to a very basic question about the nature of community structure and leadership processes: is there an overlap between the formal and the informal structure? This question really asks whether a person identified as a neighborhood activist is also likely to be an officer of a voluntary association. A second way to look at this is whether officers of voluntary associations know neighborhood activists and vice versa. These questions go to the fundamental issue of the extent to which the leadership structure of a community forms a cohesive structure. There may be a wide variety of individuals holding different leadership roles, but each of these may form separate pyramids, disparate in character, independent of but parallel to one another.

Let us consider the first form of overlap between formal and informal structure, where the same individual performs as a neighborhood activist and as an officer in a voluntary association. In terms of the black and white samples in Detroit, we find that 1 out of every 6 officers in black voluntary associations is also identified as a neighborhood activist. By contrast, this is true of about 1 out of 3 officers in white organizations. *The likelihood that a person will play the role of neighborhood activist and officer of an organization is half as great in the black as in the white community.* Overall, about 5 percent of the total sample of black respondents performed a dual role of being both an officer and activist. In contrast, we found that about 13 percent of the respondents in our white sample played this dual role.

In chart 2 we have summarized the ways in which an organization with members living in a given neighborhood might be linked to that

CHART 2

Potential Linkages
Between Voluntary Associations and Local Neighborhoods

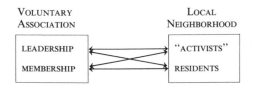

setting. As we have indicated in schematic fashion there are multiple forms of interaction. That setting in which all forms are present would have the most cohesive leadership structure. At the same time only one type of linkage might appear. It may also happen that a given neighborhood lacks all of the ties that are shown in chart 2 between formal and informal structures of leadership.

Given the basic model of linkages we can now distinguish a series of different ways in which organizations relate to the structure of a neighborhood. As we have already noted, the most basic or minimum form of linkage is simply that of organizations which have an exclusively neighborhood membership—residents of the area are the main participants. As earlier discussion has noted, this is somewhat more likely to be true in the black heterogeneous neighborhood. Another way to state this finding is that where organizations exist they are usually delimited by neighborhood boundaries.

In chart 3 we have selected a set of situations which illustrate the ways in which formal organizations of a voluntary variety relate to local neighborhoods. This is not an exhaustive set of theoretical possibilities. Instead it is based on the data obtained from black and white neighborhoods in the Detroit study. At the top is the least "coherent" pattern where leaders of organizations are seldom named as neighborhood activists, and few activists are leaders or members of voluntary associations. The pattern listed in the second position, which we' have named "grass roots outreach," exists where a number of neighborhood activists are also officers of associations. What this pattern essentially means is that formal organizations located in a neighborhood have been able to tap the "infrastructure" of the area to form its recruits for leadership roles.

In the third pattern from the top of chart 3 we have a situation where neighborhood activists are drawn largely from the ranks of voluntary association officers. The effect of this is to create a dependency of the infrastructure of the neighborhood on the persons trained and experienced as organization leaders. The implication of such a pattern should be seen as totally undesirable from the standpoint of the neighborhood, given the fact that voluntary associations and their leaders are not dominated by persons committed to the values and interests of the neighborhood. "Co-optation" then may mean a close working relationship between formal and informal systems, but it also permits manipulation of the latter system—or at least may limit its independence.

CHART 3

Types of Associational-Neighborhood Linkages

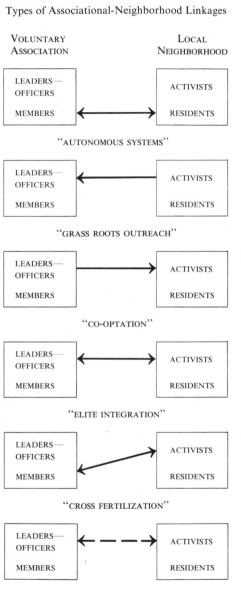

The "elite integration" pattern involves a coalescence of leadership that is symmetrical: neighborhood activists are often drawn from the ranks of organizational officers and vice versa. There is an interchange of influence but it is concentrated at the top. Among the white survey sample, more than twice the number of persons were both activists and officers in local voluntary associations as compared to the black sample.

In the fifth pattern of linkage, "cross-fertilization," members of associations frequently have the role of neighborhood activists. This means that the formal and informal structures of neighborhood are coordinated, but in a manner which avoids the danger either of cooptation by the formal structure or a mere "meeting of minds" of the elites of both systems.

In the "indirect interlock" we have depicted a situation in which formal and informal neighborhood structures are tied together, but only in terms of the knowledge of one system by members of the other. In particular, when respondents in Detroit said they "knew of someone who was active in getting things done in the neighborhood," this provided intersystem linkage. It is a more tenuous and perhaps more distant form of coordination than several of the others described.

There is perhaps some virtue in keeping an "arm's length" between formal and informal structures. This is a point made in another context by Litwak and Meyer in their "balance theory" of organizations.[6] Their argument essentially is that groups often need to be somewhat distant from one another for each to perform in the best manner, given their particular unique virtues. In other words, if the informal structure of neighborhood activists can be drawn upon by the formal structure, this can mean a more effective process for diffusing the message or advancing the goals of the group. But if the activist, while known, stays somewhat clear of being identified directly as a member of a formal group, then greater trust and flexibility in leadership vis-à-vis this informal system may result.

In chart 4 we have related the special types of linkage between formal and informal structures of neighborhoods. Our research in Detroit shows clear trends based on the racial composition and status diversity of the local area. Homogeneous areas, regardless of race, tend to manifest patterns of "indirect interlock" and "grass roots outreach." The white homogeneous neighborhoods show the greatest variety of linking patterns—three out of the six. White heterogeneous areas use different patterns from homogeneous black or white neighborhoods

CHART 4

Relationships of Detroit Research Findings to Types of
Linkage Between Voluntary Associations
and Local Neighborhoods

TYPE OF NEIGHBORHOOD	TYPE OF LINKAGE
White Homogeneous	"Cross Fertilization" "Indirect Interlock" "Grass Roots Outreach"
White Heterogeneous	"Co-optation" "Elite Integration"
Black Homogeneous	"Grass Roots Outreach" "Indirect Interlock"
Black Heterogeneous	"Autonomous"

and they show two styles of system "coherence," whereas similarly heterogeneous black areas manifest only the "autonomous"—essentially a minimal intersystem linkage (see Appendix, tables 24A and 25A).

The patterns found in the Detroit research do not define ideal modes nor do they indicate when a given pattern is preferable. But the difference in the modes by which neighborhoods link formally and informally underscores the need to understand the *potential* regarding programs and means of neighborhood interventions, either by indigenous groups or those seeking to reach local residents with given services or ideas. Our discussion also points out the implications of socioeconomic diversity and the special role it plays in connection with race patterns.

The Interlink between Neighborhoods.   Just as we have pointed out in a number of instances the duality of formal and informal leadership as it may coexist within the same neighborhood, so we must now examine the question of whether there are extensive or limited ties between leaders *across different neighborhoods*. In order to respond to this kind of inquiry, our Detroit data must be focused on the sample of organizations in which we asked active leaders to give us descriptions of what occurred within their associations.

We included in the special "leaders" sample a number of questions about where the people in the organizations lived. We found some important differences between black and white organizations in the extent to which the membership of organizations was reported to be exclusively from the local neighborhood. Thus for both heterogeneous and homogeneous black neighborhoods, there was a greater tendency for all members of these groups to live exclusively in the local neighborhood. Homogeneous white neighborhoods had the highest proportion of cases in which most people in organizations lived outside of the local neighborhood.

The general pattern of the local neighborhood is not surprising, given the character of organizations in black communities—block clubs, PTAs, and other groups with a clearly neighborhood focus. Some fundamental differences arise which reflect differences based on neighborhood setting. Thus 2 out of 5 organizations in black homogeneous areas have at least some nonneighborhood members compared to only 1 out of 5 groups in heterogeneous areas. Differences among the white sample follow a similar pattern. In both instances heterogeneity of neighborhood means a more isolated group membership.

In addition to the question about members' residences, the extent to which leadership of organizations had contacts with others outside the neighborhood becomes a useful measure of linkages. Here we found that in general all black organizations, regardless of whether they were in a homogeneous or heterogeneous neighborhood, were reported as being less active outside the neighborhood. At the same time, some important differences in both black and white neighborhoods occurred on the issue of heterogeneity. We find from our Detroit data that officers of organizations located in a homogeneous black neighborhood are more likely to be active outside of the neighborhood than those located in black heterogeneous neighborhoods. Of all group officers the organizational leader in a black heterogeneous neighborhood is least likely to be also active in a group outside of that local setting. What we have found in the Detroit data is the extent to which participation in an organization by an active period tends to *preclude* participation across neighborhood boundaries where that setting is heterogeneous. Moreover, this pattern is particularly evident in black neighborhoods that are status diverse.

Organizational Linkages. In addition to questions about the overlap in member participation as well as residential patterns, we gathered data about contacts that one organization had with groups or individuals outside of their immediate organization. For example, how often did their group meet with another group? To what extent were there meetings with important government officials or important community representatives? Were there instances where meetings from one neighborhood group were held in which somebody from another neighborhood group spoke? How often were there simultaneous meetings held with other groups? Were there joint fund raising efforts? And finally, was their local organization part of some larger structure?

When we look at the pattern of black and white neighborhoods we find that, in general, black organizations in homogeneous neighborhoods were more likely to have a range of contacts and exchanges with groups and individuals outside of the local setting than those in heterogeneous neighborhoods. In other words, holding intergroup meetings, meetings with public officials, holding joint meetings, joint fund raising efforts were all more often found where the black organization was in a homogeneous neighborhood. No such instances occurred in neighborhood settings for white organizations.

A majority of the groups whose officers were interviewed were affiliated with larger organizations. This proportions was similar in black neighborhoods regardless of type. But organizations in black heterogeneous neighborhoods were highly isolated. As will be recalled from earlier analysis we found that black organizations in heterogeneous neighborhoods were very selective in their membership and therefore were isolated from the local neighborhood.

Taking into account all of these patterns we can describe "compound" isolation of black groups in heterogeneous neighborhoods. It is based on little contact within the neighborhood and limited exchanges with groups outside of the neighborhood. In outlining the extent to which one neighborhood group has some formal relationship with another neighborhood group, we of course have identified a particular kind of linkage that may occur across neighborhoods.

But what about the more informal dimensions of formal organization ties? In other words, the fact that a leader in one group may happen to belong to another group or may happen to know individuals outside of a particular organization to which they belong. In probing these kinds of questions three measures were used: (a) whether leaders had to avoid belonging to other groups so as not to divide their loyalty, (b) whether there were influential individuals outside of the neighborhood with whom people had contact, or (c) whether there were forms of coalition with other groups. We found the following: in the black heterogeneous neighborhood we found that leaders had a slightly greater tendency to avoid belonging to other groups and there was no evidence of coalition with other organizations outside of the neighborhood. This pattern emphasizes the extent to which, both formally and informally, the leadership and total organization of black neighborhood groups could be generally more isolated when found in a heterogeneous rather than in a homogeneous setting.

Internal Status Differences and Interorganizational Linkage.   Our analysis of organizations also focused on measures of internal status conflict within a group. To the extent that such status conflict is a product of the reliance upon keeping out individuals who may have different perspectives, it might be argued that one way to avoid such conflict is to limit membership to the local setting. But if we look at organizations with high status conflict, the existence of such divisions may be a result of having a very broadly based constituency. In fact, this turns out to be precisely the case. In both black and white neighborhoods, organizations in which all members reportedly live in the neighborhood are most likely to be those high status conflict groups. At the same time we found that the black organizations which had high status conflict were more likely to be composed exclusively of neighbors than were the white organizations of high status conflict.

In the sample of black organizations we find that high status conflict in an organization is more likely to be associated with its officers being active outside or in other groups than where there is low status conflict. No such pattern prevails for white organizations. When we look at the mechanisms of formal intergroup contact, we find that there is a pattern of high status conflict black groups being in a situation where they do seek contacts with other groups. There is a similar pattern among white organizations but it is less pronounced.

On the informal side, we find with high status conflict there is a tendency in black organizations to say that leaders ought to avoid contact with other groups so as not to "divide their loyalty." This pattern is reversed for white organizations.

The internal structure of a black organization, as well as the neighborhood setting, tends to play a major role in the extent to which such organizations are free of sources of resistance to coalition building as well as knowledge and awareness about what is occurring in other neighborhoods. Our data indicate that black organizations and their leaders are frequently placed in situations which pose a conflict between internal group effectiveness and their capacity to link up both with the informal leaders in the local neighborhood and the formal organizations which exist outside of the neighborhood.

Reviewing the Findings on Leadership

What we have identified in terms of our Detroit data is the significance which the neighborhood context plays in determining what kind of leadership is to be found in a community. In particular we have pointed to the existence of at least two levels of community leadership. One is based on the officers and active members of various kinds of voluntary associations. These people are seen as forming the backbone of many community efforts. In a recent analysis, Olsen[7] points out that there are at least six different kinds of community roles which can be identified: those to whom he refers as "activists" and "communicators" are persons who are engaged in organized efforts or whose values are communicated to others.

This particular middle level of community power represents a major source of the isolated individual and the very top formal leadership of the community—elected representatives and leaders of major groups that cut across neighborhoods. Our analysis of Detroit has pointed out that in the middle levels of community leadership there are not only two types of persons who can be identified, but that the significance of these separate structures must be recognized as a basis for defining the character of any community. *Our Detroit data underscore differences in the way in which various leadership roles are performed in the black ghetto as compared with the white neighborhoods in our study.*

We have found that a significant diffusion of power prevails in black neighborhoods. The pattern of multiple leadership roles, the tendency—particularly in heterogeneous neighborhoods—for one type of leadership segment to be separated from another, represents a major characteristic of the structure of influence as we found it in our data.

The implications are extremely significant for mobilization of community power and influence. They suggest that in the black community there is a duality of local leadership and that the knitting together of the informal leader and the person who has a role in an organization is less frequently a natural pattern of neighborhoods. Therefore, to the extent to which mobilization of the community depends on access to both formal and informal leadership, the task is less easily accomplished in the black ghetto as compared with white areas.

Furthermore our data refute the notion that the black community is devoid of local leadership. The problems of community structure which seem to prevail in the black community are not the result of a lack of available resources but paradoxically to some extent are the result of the very multiplicity of leadership roles in the black ghetto. The persistence of a strong role for informal leaders, particularly in heterogeneous neighborhoods, is juxtaposed against the pyramidal interlink structure of formal and informal leadership found in white homogeneous neighborhoods of our Detroit study. The black community, in terms of our present study, is characterized by the extensity of leadership structures, the diffuseness of the linkage of one form of leadership and another, and the greater likelihood that individuals who are active and significant in terms of one definition of leadership, may not be active or significant in terms of another. This pattern of independent sources of influence and power, particularly as they are found in black heterogeneous neighborhoods, becomes a basic way to characterize the community structure of the black ghetto.

Some Policy Implications. The problems inherent in a "pluralistic power structure" represent major considerations for policy-makers as well as those in the local community itself. While there is a great deal of interest in political theory circles now about the notion of pluralism and the interest in maintaining open decision-making, we have evidence from our Detroit study that the very diversity of decision-making processes that characterize black communities may in fact be a source of dissipating the power base of the black ghetto. Policy decisions which suggest increasing the number of indigenous leaders, the utilization of local officers of organizations, and the tapping of informal neighborhood reputational leaders therefore become strategies fraught with danger. For in the very process of mobilizing the diverse and rich sources of leadership in the black community, the resulting cross-purposes with which such structures tend to operate may delay, subvert, or seriously undermine effective action.

The policy problem frequently is not one of seeking to tap the leadership or to develop a capacity for influence and action in the organizations and the individuals found in the local neighborhood, but instead it is to seek a more effective link-up and to correlate the diversity of structures and processes of leadership that may already exist. It is not fundamentally a question of *developing* leadership as much as it is one of *coordinating* that leadership. For without such efforts, the "natural" processes of fractionalization or diffusing of leadership patterns in black neighborhoods can only result in a paralysis of action.

Action Strategy Implications

We began this chapter with a discussion of leadership roles. We have relied heavily on our analysis of the Detroit data to point out what seemed to be some of the structural differences in the pattern of leadership as it occurs at the middle level of political organization, that is, the informal neighborhood activist and the officer of a voluntary association. In identifying the richness and variety of such leadership resources, we have also pointed out what may represent sharply different strategies of organization in the black ghetto as compared with either the low-income white neighborhood or the middle class white community. Selective mobilization, the defining of particular roles for these, rather than the effort to bring together the totality of leadership resources may often be called for to achieve effective and efficient decision-making.

By carefully defining the character of the problem at hand it may become necessary to differentiate which *kind of leadership structure* is to be activated to solve a given problem. If the issue, for example, is one concerned with cooperation between organizations located in one neighborhood versus another, it is clear that many of the formal structures which exist in local black areas are not likely to have easy access to other organizations. Thus particular efforts to create coalition must be introduced. At the same time, there is evidence that, on the informal level of leadership, there may well be a great deal of contact both between individuals active in organizations and those outside the organizations. In fact, the same individual may be able to take the goal of an organization and carry it to individuals who are not active in that particular group. Furthermore, such individuals may in fact have contacts beyond their immediate local neighborhood. Evidence from our Detroit study shows, for example, that the neighborhood activist in the black community is likely to have fairly extensive nonneighborhood informal contacts, at least more likely than his white counterpart. And that when such an individual belongs to an organization he or she is more likely to be in organizations that do not simply include neighbors, but other persons as well. The neighborhood activist in the black community is someone who can often be a better link with another neighborhood and with individuals beyond the local setting than is possible for the officer of a voluntary association.

At the same time, we find that the person who is both an officer in a voluntary association and an activist, is a particularly crucial or pivotal individual in any kind of community leadership process. We have found that such persons are less likely to exist in the black community than in the white community. The fragility of the role of simultaneously being both a neighborhood activist and a voluntary association officer thus becomes very evident. Yet the very absence of individuals who play this dual function pinpoints the great need for the development of these kinds of leaders.

Thus local organizations might deliberately try to recruit such persons as members of their organizations or to ascertain, when expanding the membership, whether an individual has a reputation in his local neighborhood for being an active and effective individual.

By describing those kinds of leadership roles more prevalent in the black community than in the white community, by indicating the kind of gaps which appear to be found in community leadership structures, we can pinpoint the roles of community leadership which are critical and need to be cultivated.

Our analysis of the Detroit data has indicated the richness of leadership resources that exist in the black community and the extent to which such resources can be tapped. We have noted both the gaps in types of leadership roles and the strengths which are reflected in terms of what might be effective bases of leadership.

The existence of particular kinds of leadership structures in the black ghetto may not be viewed as a situation which must inevitably be reproduced. However, as we have noted throughout our discussion, the forces of social compression as they operate in the black community tend to produce a set of critical issues which must be confronted by individuals and organizations operating within the context of community life.

The most visible expression or focus of social compression is often defined by critical individual leadership dilemmas. We have discussed the sources of such dilemmas and have brought the larger structural elements down to the point of describing the kinds of individual positions that leadership must fill. This may indeed require a reconceptualization of what kinds of social characteristics are most likely to result in individuals being effective as community leaders.

Chapter VII

Alienation and Activism in the Black Ghetto

The ghetto is ferment, paradox, conflict, and dilemma. Yet within its pervasive pathology exists a surprising human resilience. The ghetto is hope, it is despair. . . . It is aspiration for change, and it is apathy. It is vibrancy, it is stagnation. It is courage, and it is defeatism. It is cooperation and concern, and it is suspicion, competitiveness, and rejection. It is the surge toward assimilation, and it is alienation and withdrawl within the protective walls of the ghetto.

>   Kenneth B. Clark,
>   *Dark Ghetto* (New York: Harper and Row, 1965), pp. 11–12

THERE ARE PERHAPS as many ways to define the term "alienation" as there are social scientists who purport to analyze it. So much of contemporary social commentary and journalistic discussion alludes to individual expressions of alienation that efforts to narrow and specify the meaning of this "catchall" term have not kept pace.[1] What is particularly disturbing from the point of view of community analysis is that "alienation" connotes invariably something which is pathological, harmful as a psychological state for the individual, undermining for the group as a basis of cohesion and esprit de corps.

I wish to take a rather different view of alienation. Seen in its historic role as the expression of injustice, oppression, and dissatisfaction with the existing values and structures of society, alienation is in fact a major force in constructive social change. I regard it as a sign of hope within a community when we mean specifically that individuals learn about their environment and focus upon its failings; this should be seen as a sign of hope and not despair within a community. Where individuals do not perceive their situation in other than immediate, eyeball-to-eyeball terms, contentment is merely a sign of isolation, not of well-being.

Equating Alienation with the Black Ghetto: Some Paradoxes

The theme of alienation as applied to the black ghetto may call forth images of young militants, rioters, civil rights activists, or "street dudes." These are stereotypes of the kind that tend to appeal to the mass media image makers. It certainly is easier to try to deal with alienation in these individual terms or in most dramatic forms of crime, violence, protest, or even mental illness. What characterizes so much of the recent outpouring of analyses about black ghetto "alienation" is the diversified gambit of its expression—virtually any behavior is ascribed to the rubric of "alienation."

This brings us to an important question: given the thesis of ghetto life generating various types of individual alienation, how can the specific form it takes for one person but not another be explained? Does it make any sense, for example, to say in the same breath that ghetto riots are due to the "alienation" of younger blacks and so is the relatively low voting turnout in local and state elections of this same group? How can a connection be made between the two phenomena? We could of course draw a parallel in terms of a hypothesis about "revolutionary consciousness." It is possible to argue that withdrawal of many blacks from the established democratic institutions of the black and white community and their refusal to riot amount to "alienation within the system."

But there is a missing link in this type of argumentation. How is it that particular individuals come to the point of taking a "system blame" versus a "self-blame" approach to life? What are the sources for such perspectives? Does participation in the life of the black ghetto create such attitudes? Or is it rather that those who are at the periphery of the social structure of the black ghetto become the visibly alienated?

William Gamson's essay on *Power and Discontent* provides a useful framework for approaching the question raised by black ghetto alienation. In his discussion Gamson suggests, for example, that the concept of political alienation deals with two often confounded elements: political trust and political efficacy. According to his argument, these may be defined as follows: "The efficacy dimension . . . refers to people's perceptions of their ability to influence; the trust dimension refers to their perception of the necessity for influence."[2] He further states:

Feelings of low efficacy and feeling that the government is not being run in one's own interest are of course likely to be found together. If one feels he cannot contribute significant inputs he is likely also to feel unhappy with the outputs. But this is an empirical hypothesis which might prove false under some conditions.[3]

The dimension of trust may lead to a high degree of nonparticipation according to Gamson's analysis. And it is related to the idea that nonvoting or other signs of inactivity can "be a sign of confidence as well as of alienation."[4] High trust in authorities implies some lack of the necessity for influencing them.

In this situation for example a number of studies by political scientists show that a maximum voting turnout is not necessarily the healthiest sign of a democracy. Where extremist groups of the right and left are brought into the arena and mobilized, the very fabric of a society is often torn asunder. Consequently, the notion of a relatively moderate degree of participation is viewed as the most desirable outcome and either extremely low or extremely high participation seen as indicators of the breakdown of the social order.

In contrast to the view of what occurs when there is a high degree of trust, Gamson suggests that:

Failure and frustration are frequently debilitating and demoralizing and increases in discontent can have an effect that is the opposite from mobilizing people. More specifically, a combination of high sense of political efficacy and low political trust is the optimum combination for mobilization, a belief that influence is possible and necessary.[5]

Support for the thesis elaborated by Gamson is given by two independent studies of black community activists. John Forward and Jay Williams (1970) found that young black who are high on militancy attitudes "have very strong beliefs in their ability to control events in their own lives and to shape their own future. . . . This radically new sense of self-efficacy in militants is juxtaposed with an increasingly realistic perception of those external barriers of discrimination, prejudice and exploitation which block any chance of actualizing their capabilities and their realizing their aspirations."[6] Forward and Williams go on to suggest that "the combination of a heightened sense of personal effectiveness and the shift from self to system blame, may help to explain the willingness of young ghetto militants to resort to violence as a means of forcing a change in the opportunity structure which at present excludes them."[7]

In a study of the Newark riot, Jeffery Paige (1971) employed the Gamson concepts and concluded that "rioters were most often found among the dissident—those high on political information and low on trust in the government."[8] In discussing the basis of riot behavior Paige argues that:

Extremist political tactics, like other forms of politics, require interest in government but, unlike conventional forms (of participation) imply that the government is fundamentally untrustworthy. . . . The relationship between efficacy, trust and political participation depends not only on the characteristics of the group but on the relationship between the group and the political system. A knowledgeable citizenry with an unresponsive regime is likely to turn to radical or violent tactics, while the same level of knowledge in a responsive system would lead to loyalty and conventional political action.[9]

In other words, the increased awareness which may occur by belonging to organizations and being active in a community can provide the basis of "alienation" where such involvement shows that the "system" is unresponsive, corrupt, or ineffective.

Paige also defines two situations which result in other than radical action mobilization:

The low efficacy, low trust situation produces an alienated orientation which would lead to withdrawal from any active political participation. . . . The low efficacy, high trust situation also suggests a passive adjustment although in this case the population believes that the government is basically run in the best interests.[10]

In other words "passive alienation" can be easily confused with the inaction which results from having no reason to question the actions of government.

The Gamson-Paige formulation provides a means to clarify two problems of analyzing alienation: (1) the relationship of one form of alienation to another—sometimes taking action and in other instances refusing to participate in some active way; (2) the conditions under which a given form of alienation produces a specific behavior. Thus Gamson's dimensions of trust and efficacy are aspects of "system alienation"—they relate to the political system of the community or larger society. The more traditional studies of anomie and normlessness usually deal with general psychological states—interpersonal isolation and integration.

Many analyses of the black ghetto as well as other "alienated" communities have tended to confuse the "system" and "personal" levels of analysis. Both are important but each has significantly different implications for understanding human behavior as well as the nature of social action.

A Model for Evaluating the Effects of System Alienation. The formulation discussed by Gamson and Paige provides an orientation to the conditions under which an individual's "alienation" is associated with greater or lesser participation in the political process. In his analysis of ghetto rioters, Paige applied this approach in order to refute the notion that hopelessness and irrationality formed basic motivations in the behavior of blacks who were active in urban disorders of the 1960s. Let us now incorporate such a schema in the more fundamental task of relating ghetto social structure to general political mobilization. How well do these notions fit our data on the Detroit black ghetto?

In chart 5 the basic mode of analysis is presented. Here we are dealing with the two notions of "trust" and "efficacy." The first of these ideas focuses on the products or "outputs" of government or the institutions of society. If the individual feels that such structures can be assumed to hold his own interests to some reasonable degree, then the extent of political action is an affirmation or reaffirmation of his legitimization of those institutions. Efficacy is a term that describes the "inputs" that an individual can have in the political process. To the degree that governmental agencies are responsive, interested, and take action, then the individual may exercise influence using established channels such as city agencies, civic groups, voting, and participation in voluntary associations.

By taking the four possible combinations of trust and efficacy, Paige describes a typology of characteristic orientations of political systems. Chart 5 reproduces the formulation in which four situations are defined: (a) "both efficacy and trust are high . . . (Allegiants) feel both that the government will be run in their interests and that they can influence it when necessary," (b) "an alienated orientation which would lead to withdrawal from any active political participation," (c) "a passive adjustment. . . . Demands are seldom presented by interest groups so that responsiveness is not an important issue. . . .

CHART 5

Relationship of Trust and Efficacy to Political Orientation,
Behavior of Regime, and Nature of Political System

| | | TRUST | |
		High	Low
EFFICACY	High	Allegiant "Democratic"	Dissident "Unstable"
	Low	Subordinate "Traditional"	Alienated "Totalitarian"

SOURCE: Jeffery M. Paige, "Political Orientation and Riot Participation," *American Sociological Review*, XXXVI (October 1971), p. 812.

The ruler maintains an image of beneficent paternalism . . . ," and (d) [where] "the government is regarded as untrustworthy and there is a feeling that something can and should be done about it . . . radical actions aimed at changing the system are likely to result."[11]

As formulated by Paige the four cells shown in chart 5 may be applied to any population. In the case of the sample of black and white Detroiters we utilized the scheme shown in the abstract to describe the individual adaptations of individuals to the larger social system. In this sense the Paige formulation is a kind of schematic of communities' mobilization potential. In the case of patterns of black ghetto responses to political activism, this approach allows us to distinguish orientations that have frequently been lumped under the rubric of "alienated" or "militant." Instead we can now ask the question: does being active in the political process mean a high degree of integration or potential integration into that "system" or is it a reflection of protest against the injustice and unresponsiveness of that "system"?

Using our interviews in Detroit we constructed indices of "trust" and "efficacy." On the first concept we utilized a series of questions which asked people to react to the behavior of the government toward such topics as the assassination of Martin Luther King, John Kennedy, covering up the truth about Flying Saucers, and a CIA plot to assassinate Malcolm X. A second index was built around responses to the question of whether people working in various institutions were responsive to and interested in "the people like yourself." Organizations mentioned included state and federal government, banks, public schools, police, unions, automobile companies and welfare agencies as well as others. The more often people said such groups had little interest in people like themselves, the higher the score of "powerlessness" or lack of efficacy.

In table 2 we have indicated how black and white respondents in the Detroit sample were grouped according to the fourfold pattern of adaptation to system functioning. Let us pause to examine the pattern reflected from the empirical data. First, we note that most persons, black and white, in the Detroit sample are "Allegiants"— they believe that the government tells the truth and that government and other major institutions are responsive to people like themselves. In fact this is somewhat more true of blacks than whites. Second, about the same proportion of blacks as whites are in the "Alienated" category—feel they are inefficacious and distrust the government.

The important differences between blacks and whites in the Detroit

TABLE 2

**Distribution of Blacks and Whites in
Relation to "System" Adaptation**

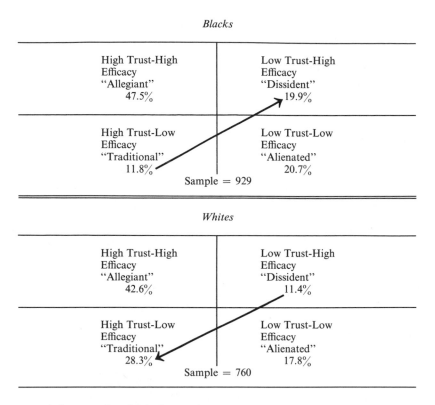

Blacks

High Trust-High Efficacy "Allegiant" 47.5%	Low Trust-High Efficacy "Dissident" 19.9%
High Trust-Low Efficacy "Traditional" 11.8%	Low Trust-Low Efficacy "Alienated" 20.7%

Sample = 929

Whites

High Trust-High Efficacy "Allegiant" 42.6%	Low Trust-High Efficacy "Dissident" 11.4%
High Trust-Low Efficacy "Traditional" 28.3%	Low Trust-Low Efficacy "Alienated" 17.8%

Sample = 760

sample have to do with being "Dissident" versus taking a "Traditional" stance of accepting powerlessness as legitimate. Thus we find that about 1 in 5 blacks feels that the government is not to be trusted and that individuals can have some impact on government and major social institutions. This is true of 1 out of 9 whites. By contrast, more than 1 out of 4 whites feel that the government is to be trusted and that they cannot expect to be paid attention to. Less than half this proportion of blacks take such a view.

What our Detroit study confirms is that the feeling of Dissident "alienation" or activism is a spirit more to be found in the black ghetto than in white areas. At the same time the acceptance of a kind of paternalistic fatalism or passivity is found less often in the black ghetto than in white neighborhoods. These patterns fit what Paige found in regard to the orientation of the black rioter. It suggests further that the spark of ghetto "rebellion" lies deeper in the social structure of the black urban community than a particular expression of dramatic, visible upheaval.

Activism versus Atavism

Is the fact of a difference in the "political orientation" of blacks versus whites in Detroit an expression of unstructured radicalism or is it a major basis of community mobilization to take effective action? Let us briefly review the Gamson-Paige formulation and see why the data we have presented from Detroit are a valuable base line. Since the notion of either the Allegiant person or the Alienated person both suggest low activism, holding either view should be associated with low levels of community activism. Traditional persons in this same formulation may be seen to have little motivation to act since they accept the system as legitimate and feel besides that they will not be heeded should they seek to become involved. That leaves the Dissident person with the highest probability of taking action, local or national.

Do the predictions about the patterns of adaptation and the level of mobilization hold true in our Detroit data? To answer this question we compared persons in the black and white sample who had different scores on trust and efficacy in terms of the following expression of social action: (a) helping neighbors, (b) belonging to organizations with neighbors, (c) contacting city agencies to express concerns about problems, and (d) voting in the national election that occurred prior to the survey. In table 3 the patterns correlating all of these variables are shown.

We find that in almost every instance the connection between a particular kind of system adaptation and the level of social action is different for blacks compared to whites. Thus we find that whites who are most loyal to the "system" are highly active in it. For blacks, those who are Dissident are most active. The exception is contacting city agencies. Among blacks Traditional or paternalistic orientations mean little involvement in the local community or beyond. For whites there is average or higher involvement. To be Alienated in the black ghetto means almost as much activism as to be Dissident. The same orientation in the white community means withdrawal.

So in most ways we have found that the relationship between holding particular attitudes about the "system" results in different behaviors when it is a white versus a black individual involved. One

TABLE 3

**Forms of System Adaptation
and Level of Social Action**

Blacks

"Allegiant" Average amount of mutual aid with neighbors Below average number of members in neighbor-linked groups Low contact with city agencies Below average voting in presidential election	"Dissident" High mutual aid with neighbors High number of memberships in neighbor-linked organizations Low contact with city agencies Average voting in presidential election
"Traditional" Low on all activism measures	"Alienated" Average mutual aid with neighbors Above average number of neighbor-linked organizations High contact with city agencies Average voting in presidential election

Whites

"Allegiant" Above average on all activism measures	"Dissident" Below average on all activism measures
"Traditional" Above average on all activism measures	"Alienated" Below average on all activism measures

implication of these findings is that theories of community action which may apply to whites do not appear to be valid for blacks. Perhaps more significant in terms of focus on the social structure of the black ghetto is that participation, especially in the neighborhood, is largely a function of Dissident and Alienated orientations. In other words, our Detroit data show that whites become active in their community as a direct result of feeling they can trust that system—*even if they are not likely to be heard.*

The Detroit findings provide evidence for a notion of "victimization" consciousness as an important basis of community action in the black ghetto. When individuals come to view the "system" as unlikely to produce "payoffs" or where "inputs" are not likely to have an impact on institutions, then in the black ghetto this is associated with a high level of community participation. The policy implications are worth noting at this point. First of all it seems that isolation from the black community is partially a function of loyalty to the external institutions of the national government and more local "establishment" institutions. Consequently if one increases the level of local neighborhood involvement, it does not follow that individuals will then feel more tied in the larger society. The opposite may hold true. Furthermore, if we see efforts at "mobilizing" the poor as a product of their lack of contact with institutions and their alienation a result of not knowing how the larger society functions, then such interventions had best be confined to white rather than black neighborhoods. For our Detroit data imply that in the case of the Alienated black ghetto dweller it is the unresponsiveness and perceived cupidity of these very institutions— based on some direct contact—that generates such attitudes.

The implication should also be drawn that such orientations apply to the larger black as well as to the white social structure. For it is in the context of local neighborhood involvement that alienation from the larger black as well as from the white community is fostered. In the case of the Dissident activist the concentration of the local milieu is even more pronounced than in the case of the Alienated activist in the black ghetto.

Two Paths to Activism: Tracing the Sources. In noting how both Dissident and Alienated black ghetto dwellers show higher levels of social activism than other blacks, we have raised the question about whom the two groups represent and whether different forces produce them. Here we can trace the particular social structural features of black ghettoes that we have discussed earlier and show their impact. Let us first take the issue of local neighborhood. Our Detroit data show that the Dissident is more likely to emerge in the setting of the homogeneous neighborhood. By contrast the Alienated black activist is more likely to come out of a heterogeneous local context. The result is that the latter type of neighborhood may produce a person who is more willing to act as a "defender" of the local area—to rely on neighborhood informal or formal organization. This produces a good anchor point for community action but does not give much support to "offensive" efforts—contacting the larger black or white institutions to generate protest or pressure for change.

To further underscore this difference we find that in the Parochial and Diffuse type of black neighborhood Alienation is more frequently found than the Dissident orientation. In Stepping-Stone and Transitory areas there is likely to be a larger proportion of Dissident than Alienated persons. This latter point is of interest since findings from the author's 1967 study of ghetto rioting in Detroit show that these same types of neighborhoods also had the highest riot involvement.

In Anomic neighborhoods both Dissidents and Alienated persons are a smaller proportion of the population, as is the case in Integral areas. Thus the activist, Dissident or Alienated, is found more often in those kinds of black neighborhoods which are neither totally locked into the larger society nor totally isolated from local community participation.

In our discussion of "status inconsistency" in chapter 3, we noted that being discrepant from local neighborhoods, peers or from the larger status norms of society had important implications for black community participation. Our Detroit data also suggest that each type of status inconsistency results in a different stance toward activism. Thus the individual whose socioeconomic status is different from the typical resident of the local neighborhood is more likely to be a Dissident activist as compared to an Alienated activist. By contrast, that black ghetto dweller whose socioeconomic status is typical of his neighbors, but shows a pattern of inconsistency using general patterns of the total community, is more likely to be the Alienated activist. However all forms of status inconsistency are linked to activism.

In terms of organizational participation there is yet another pattern which accounts for one type of activist versus another. The black ghetto dweller who is a member of some organizations where neighbors are seen and some where neighbors do not belong is significantly more likely to fall into the Dissident group than other persons. In other words, the pattern of splitting one's ties between the local neighborhood and the larger black and white community brings about a perspective in which activism means a feeling of effectiveness but coupled with distrust of the larger society.

By contrast that individual in the black ghetto who belongs to organizations made up of exclusively neighbor-linked groups is likely to be an Alienated activist, to believe that the "system" is unresponsive and that he can do little to change it. A similar pattern prevails for blacks who belong to groups which are not tied to the local neighborhood. In other words, where the individual in the black ghetto chooses either exclusively neighborhood or exclusively nonneighborhood community participation, he is more likely to be Alienated rather than Dissident in his orientation.

The Dissident Activist: A Profile of the Pivotal Change Agent. From our Detroit findings we can now reconstruct the parameters that comprise a kind of composite of forces shaping the view which Paige and others see as the "radical" or "unstable" component of black ghetto dynamics. In our own view we are concerned with identifying a matrix of elements associated with high community participation often running counter to traditional participation but not necessarily antithetical to effective community change.

The Dissident orientation in the black ghetto is a view that links the often dual allegiance of local neighborhood and larger black community. This latter concept is often more of a subjective view than a notion of geographical boundaries. It means "Black Consciousness," not simply residence in an all-black neighborhood. The Dissident activist has ties both to a local neighborhood and to structures and organizations that do not subsume the local milieu. This means that the neighborhood structure is cohesive and homogeneous enough to have organizations within its boundaries which do not focus exclusively on local neighborhood problems or recruits.

In addition, the Dissident activist, while being active in the local neighborhood, is often in socioeconomic status not on a par with his or her neighbors. In this sense the individual may have higher income, education, or occupational levels than neighbors. Sometimes the reverse is true. But the identification with the local neighborhood is one source of "creative tension" that the Dissident activist may feel. For to be "in the neighborhood" but not totally "of it" can result in desire to flee the scene of such a schism. But where the individual is able to resolve such a dilemma—one which we have argued is a structurally induced problem of black urban ghettoes—then a major function of community is fulfilled. By serving as the bridge between the local neighborhood and the larger world, the Dissident activist brings skill and spirit to the local milieu that may otherwise be lacking. The frustration and disappointment of local groups and activists who have come to expect little from their efforts can be converted by the Dissident activist into a renewed effort at challenging fixed institutions, both black and white.

It is not simply in terms of the structure of organizations and the level of participation that community change emerges, but in the determination of individuals to bring about desired reality. In the black urban ghetto such motivations and their sources would appear to be distinctive—at least compared to the experience of immigrant white groups. The very time in which the black ghetto has become the complex reality we have delineated militates against some of the more traditional ethnic styles of organization. The innovation and experimentation with forms and modes of community "institution building"[12] in the black ghetto which have emerged in recent years may grow from the same roots as urban rioting. The Dissident and Alienated stance of many blacks in urban ghettoes is not a function of media exposure or topical "urban crisis" politics. The task of harnessing such discontent is perhaps not so much the problem of the white majority as it is the first order of priority for the black community.

Chapter VIII

Social Change and the Structure of the Black Ghetto

The neighborhood is no more a small town than it is an underdeveloped country. The old Du Pont (neighborhood) Council was successful primarily because it did not try to recreate an organic community. Rather, it sought to relate the area to citywide systems.
Harold H. Weissman.
Community Councils and Community Control
(Pittsburg: University of Pittsburg Press, 1970), p. 175

Guiding Principles Emerging from our Analysis

IN PREVIOUS CHAPTERS we have focused on each of several major elements of community structure in the black ghetto. The composite of these pieces provides the picture of a distinct social system. The elements making up this mosiac are built upon the hard facts of ghetto growth, differentiation, geographic and social mobility, as well as the economic reality of "underdevelopment" and continuous depression.[1] Many of the descriptive and analytic concepts we have utilized may be viewed as "working hypotheses." They are supported mainly by the data from our research in Detroit.

At this point we could discuss the litany of methodological and empirical problems, the limitations of our findings, and the need for further testing and validation. We certainly support the search for new concepts and future research using the same or ancillary concepts. But in a larger sense there is a core of specific prescriptions and several proscriptions that flow from the overall approach we have developed. It is the distillation of these insights to which I should now like to turn. They are, in the best sense of the term, diagnostic tools. They can also be viewed as a set of conditioning factors that need to be addressed in the design of social action or program interventions, economic, political, or interpersonal. Let us now identify three major propositions that provide a comprehensive overview of social policy assumptions relative to the black ghetto.

1. *Structural integration of the black ghetto is a more critical focal concern for social change than individual mobilization and community participation per se.*

There is very substantial research literature about the under-participation and isolation of the individual ghetto dweller. Yet exceptions to this view have begun to emerge. We also question this perspective. It conflicts at a number of points with the findings of our neighborhood analysis in Detroit.

Granted there are areas where individuals may not belong to any type of organization, where isolation of the individual is a critical problem of black community development. But our fundamental argument is that the character of many black neighborhood groups and voluntary associations is such that they serve as vehicles for effective individual participation but do not provide a nexus and interlocked structure of community power.

We have identified a number of the specific aspects of this critical pattern of individual participation without effective neighborhood integration into the black ghetto as a whole or with respect to access to white institutions and white-dominated community resources. The index of community alienation is not the involvement of the individual, but the functional role which that participation provides for the community as a whole. It is not a question of the motivations for people joining groups.

Certainly a spirit of community responsibility and desire for collective action is needed. But we need to look beyond the act of participation to the network of groups and structures which, when taken as a whole, determines the effect of each person's separate role in community life. Our index must therefore be seen as a systemic or cumulative one. The number of neighborhood groups and voluntary associations in the black ghetto is not the critical consideration. Nor is the number of groups that an individual belongs to. The question is not one of "maximum feasible or participation," but rather the capacity of groups to coordinate their activities and to devise effective structures that result in meaningful change.

Structural Isolation. Where black urban ghettoes have developed networks of social participation, on formal and informal levels, which presume a fixed and confined geographical population base, forms of organization reinforce these patterns by basing linkages on territoriality, namely, the local neighborhood.

In Detroit's black areas both homogeneous and heterogeneous neighborhoods were characterized by the fact that formal organization membership focused on neighbors. Not only did such groups contain mainly neighbors but the amount of out-of-neighborhood associational ties of those members were more limited.

Yet the pattern of isolation and parochialism was not based upon homogeneity in most cases, but instead was associated with the status diversity in a neighborhood. In other words, the conventional notion that it is the deadening similarity of the ghetto which produces a limited base for community effort must be modified.

Our Detroit analysis has shown that in black heterogeneous neighborhoods, associations are very restrictive in their recruitment of members and function only because of a highly developed degree of internal cohesion. When black organizations are found in homogeneous neighborhoods, they are less selective in their recruitment and have a higher degree of linkage with outside organizations.

Social Compression. The measures of involvement in wider political structures of the society provide the most vivid explication of such a process. Not only is the individual's adaptation in terms of active or passive alienation related to induced status dilemmas but it also involves the type of neighborhood in which he lives and the functioning of its organizations. In turn, whether blacks rely on informal helping among neighbors or make use of community services, contact city agencies, vote in elections, or a wide variety of other "community relevant" behaviors appear to depend more on these local milieux than is the case for nonghetto urban dwellers.

Black ghettoization involves a paradoxical duality. Individuals are overdependent on a highly localized resource in the local arena, and at the same time, persons who have a partial commitment to the local neighborhood may be heavily weighted with social-distancing attitudes vis-à-vis these same neighbors with whom they find themselves juxtaposed. It is therefore in this mutually enhanced alienation from the immediate locale and from the larger culture that ghettoization may be defined.

Distinctive Patterns of Social Alienation. If we use an indicator such as participation in organizations, we find many black respondents in our Detroit study showing a greater awareness of the need for system change and a lessening of inwardly directed frustration. Yet, the very success of black groups in directing attention to the sources of social discontent also serves to focus undue attention on some one particular mechanism of social action at the expense of developing other levers of social change. By elaborating a series of highly localized and neighborhood oriented groups, ghettoization serves to insulate many blacks from the institutional networks and nexuses which serve to perpetuate what is clearly the economic and political inequity between the ghetto and the rest of the urban community. It may well be argued that the focus on unity building in areas of neighborhood heterogeneity drains the energy of the leadership of many ghetto groups and serves as an unrewarding exercise for black individuals who seek social change.

Without linkage between local neighborhoods and the wider black community and, in turn, its interrelations with the dominant white social structure, much of the existing role of social participation in the ghetto is expressed only in individual mobility opportunities. At the same time other consequences flow from this pattern. It often heightens passive forms of alienation and self-estrangement. It represents the failure of ghetto organizations to provide even for purely expressive aspects of class, occupational and value consensus. Thus the social-psychological benefits of neighborhood cohesion or organizational participation must be distinguished from the gains to the community as a whole, the social structural benefits.

> 2. *The special importance of neighborhood structure in the ghetto means that efforts to ameliorate job, income, and housing problems must specifically take into account the social composition of the neighborhood and also to minimize the status and value conflicts therein.*

The rhetoric not reality of such programs as school decentralization, Model Cities Community Action Programs, and Community Development Corporations carry the theme of neighborhood power. A great deal of the discussion of these efforts and the evaluation of their effectiveness rest on fallacious assumptions about low income and ghetto communities.[2] Often these efforts have multiple and conflicting goals.[3] Providing needed social services and "organizing the poor" are often incompatible.

Our research in Detroit speaks to the issue raised in Federal, state, and local governmental efforts. To argue that the local neighborhood needs to "be organized" often means adding new structures that compete with those already operating. In other instances the mechanism of participation employs a procedure such as formal elections which may not be effective as a means of obtaining representation for all. Perhaps an even more basic flaw associated with programs of "local control" is the absence of criteria for or awareness of meaningful geographic boundaries of local neighborhoods. Our research findings in Detroit implicitly call for the careful scrutiny of "local control" and its selective rather than blanket utilization in policy formulations.

Artificially Created Geographical Units.   Black neighborhoods are created and changed by the de jure and de facto segregation policies of schools, real estate firms, and other formal and informal institutions of the dominant white society. Two dilemmas emerge in this artificial mobility of blacks in urban areas: the excessively heterogeneous character of the border of middle income ghetto neighborhoods and the often stifling uniformity of public housing and lower middle income housing locales. Evidence from the Detroit area research indicates that the high degree of status diversity of many black neighborhoods is reproduced in suburban black communities. Thus if large central city ghettoes show a pattern of polarization, very homogeneous or very heterogeneous neighborhoods, areas of new black settlement may carry at least one of these extremes in local community structure beyond its original source.

The ramifications of the "artificiality" pertain not only to the nature of local neighborhood cohesion and interaction, but also to the economic and political structures to be found within them. While the evidence is that black neighborhoods are no more likely to have absentee ownership than low income white areas[4], it is clear that the perception of "occupation" by such outside institutions as the police, social work agencies, and white-owned enterprises is a major source of personal and community estrangement. This belief, whether well founded or not, acts as a self-fulfilling prophecy.

Rapid residential movement in many black ghetto neighborhoods fosters both the evanescence of what is most desirable about the locale and the tenacity of decay that accompanies population instability. Francis Piven puts the issue this way: "On its own, the ghetto seems better described as an economic backwater than an economic colony, the sluggish backwater of a swift and dynamic economy.[5] Ghetto neighborhoods are bypassed by both white and black entrepreneurs. Sturdivant, in evaluating the success of Community Development Corporations, concludes that "the objective of creating a cohesive unit in the ghetto through involving a maximum number of people in the decision-making process of the community corporation is one which has proved to be largely impractical."[6]

Distinctive Types of Black Neighborhoods.   Findings from the Detroit study indicate that particular kinds of local neighborhoods occur with different frequency in white versus black population centers. It is not simply economic level, but also the forms of local associations and groups, and the way individuals view their neighborhood.

There is a general pattern in black neighborhoods for the local area of interaction to take on more important roles and to be diversified in the functions they can play. Not only do black neighborhoods serve as important centers of informal contact, but there is also a greater identification with the local neighborhood and a high reliance on the opinion of neighbors. Often the relationship between neighbors shows a greater range of difference between one black area and another than is to be found among the white areas in our study. Therefore, neighborhood as a critical determinant is expressed not only in the greater intensity with which individuals relate to that unit but also in the variety of forms which were expressed by that particular building block of community.

Status Confrontation in the Local Neighborhood.   Where spatial compression exists as a factor in community life, individuals find themselves more often in proximity and social interaction with persons who, while sharing dominant attributes of ethnicity, may differ substantially in terms of social values, status levels, and individual attributes.

At a number of points of our analysis, the particular clustering of socioeconomic statuses that individuals in the black community hold —coupled with the significance of discrepancies in such status (high education but modest income or the reverse)—play a major role in determining how individuals participate both formally and informally in the life of the black ghetto. Divergences in the measures of what is an appropriate base of status and the multiplicity of such criteria become a basic attribute of the black ghetto's social structure.

Patterns of increase in status differentiation accompanied by relatively fixed community geographical boundaries provides for increased interstratum contacts and greater difficulty in defining what are the significant bases of achieved social status.

Interlinking of Neighborhood and Organizational Patterns in the Black Ghetto.   The spatial attributes of black urban communities define patterns of formal and informal association for the constituent population. What this meant in our Detroit analysis was that neighborhoods, which were more often heterogeneous in the black ghetto, were not able to perform the wide variety of functions which the more homogeneous neighborhoods took on as significant bases on black community structure. Moreover, we found that the very characteristics of neighborhood status variations had a distinctive effect not only on the primary group but also on the formal organizational patterns found within that neighborhood. Furthermore, the social attitudes of individuals within such neighborhoods were found to be distinctive from persons living in more homogeneous settings. In addition, the very structure of organizations found in such neighborhoods also were distinctive and reflected the dynamic interplay of intra- as well as interorganizational forms. Not only structure but goals of groups in black areas were closely linked to local settings. Organizations in heterogeneous neighborhoods emphasized expressive rather than instrumental goals, were highly selective in character, and could be fundamentally defined by their residential milieu.

> 3. *Voluntary associations must be viewed as a crucial factor in strategies of community organization. This means recognizing the limitations of such organizations under conditions of heterogeneity and their peculiar and distinctive strengths.*

To what extent does the Detroit research give support for those who reflect widespread disillusionment with efforts to use voluntary associations as building blocks of community? Several issues emerge from our analysis which provide a focus for responding both to the critics of community voluntarism and to those who view voluntary associations as a panacea for ghetto ills.

Need for Specific Organizational Goals.   Since voluntary associations are more expressive of common interests rather than diffuse goals, attempts at umbrella forms of community organization must be seriously questioned. Efforts are better spent in trying to identify diverse interests in the ghetto, legitimizing them, and then maximizing goals through formal organizations having clear-cut purposes. At the same time, formal associational linkages should be avoided in the attaining of social goals where this may draw together conflicting groups who will remain united only under crisis conditions, if even then. Rejecting formal organizations as a tool for social action must be seriously considered. The failure of such organizations, notably in the lower socioeconomic groups, exacerbates social ills and the resulting product, individual alienation. Alternative methods are called for and the recognition of the limitations of voluntary associations must be tied to a realistic view of social structure in the ghetto.

Neighborhood Effects on Organizations. Where neighborhoods are heterogeneous in the black community, there are often fewer linkages between such centers and outside groups. In addition, such neighborhoods tend to lack both the range of informal and formal leadership networks found in more homogeneous black neighborhoods. But even the commitment of highly active leaders rests on an ambiguous alienation from the larger white community without any accompanying identification with the local black neighborhood or with black ethnicity per se.

In terms of overall participation in organizations, blacks are more likely to see neighbors and to meet in the local neighborhood. They are also less likely to belong to associations which do not include some neighbors. When such external participation does occur, it represents an expression of the mutually exclusive participation pattern which is present as part of "structural alienation" of the black ghetto.

Status Dilemmas and Black Organizations. Much of the data on status inconsistency suggest that both formal and informal contact with neighbors and in voluntary associations brings to the fore the status dilemmas that an incomplete or a poorly crystallized social mobility pattern induces. This pattern, while not confined to blacks, takes on a special significance within the black ghetto. In order for individuals to share some basis of status, there must be a "borrowing of status." And in this sense the evidence is that blacks turn to voluntary associations as bases for "cashing-in" on status claims or achieved social mobility.

By alternately increasing participation in organizations and at the same time reducing their memberships in neighborhood groups ghetto blacks induce a pattern of "shopping around" for participation in the most prestigious or important community group. Associational linkages may become highly restrictive of participation in order to maximize the internal cohesion and the common goals of the group or may accomodate to the heterogeneity of membership by shifting from its original goals to those which are more acceptable to the diverse membership contained within it. At the same time a greater number of black organizations show a degree of internal status conflict than was the case in white areas in our Detroit study.

Utilization of Local Leadership Resources. The role of the local neighborhood in its multivariate functions may be approached most effectively by building upon such functions and structures as they already exist. But they must be used in their indigenous forms.

Such local units cannot be transformed into convenient administrative units by drawing upon the informal leadership in these areas and making them serve as intermediaries between larger governmental efforts and the individual resident. By making this kind of linkage, the significance of the intermediate local power structure may be completely undermined. The legitimacy of the local neighborhood leader rests directly with his lack of attachment to other formal structures of government. To make them agents of such institutions is to undercut their very base of support and influence. Therefore, much that is discussed under the rubric "co-optation" becomes more comprehensible when we recognize that the problem is not one of individual motivations and role dilemmas alone, but one of the *de facto* structure of black communities.

Federal programs which in the past have sought to draw upon local leaders or which have attempted to establish new leadership structures in local neighborhoods have proven to be very ineffective for two reasons. First, they have attempted to co-opt and transform the local neighborhood leadership and thus rob it of its very legitimacy. Second, they have attempted to create a parallel and additional structure which only lengthens the chain of command and further increases the alienation of the individual. Consequently, the fallacy of centralized federal intervention in the black ghetto rests precisely on its ignoring of the diversity and variation found within local neighborhoods. At the same time, fault lies with the assumption that one is dealing with potentially disorganized areas, which, if strengthened and viewed as building blocks of community, can provide a kind of stability and efficiency which apparently is lacking in minority and low-income areas.

Given the recent upsurge in black organizations and the fact that the leadership cadre in the ghetto is, by virtue of formal education and economic affluence, likely to draw upon persons whose participation in the community is made at greater sacrifice than in the majority community, effective use of this group is essential. Overtaxed by multiple leadership roles, many higher status ghetto activists find their commitments to a single neighborhood group or special purpose organization undermined by their being in high demand in the scarce market of black ghetto leadership. The white community has the luxury of a broader category of potential participants in organizations.

Data from the Detroit study suggest that some patterns of black ghetto leadership may have some built-in advantages. The evidence of a closer interlock between formal and informal neighborhood activists, as well as the multiple roles played by many organizational officers, provides a basis for linking local and nonlocal efforts.

There would appear to be several strategies which can "stretch" and make more effective the relatively small leadership cadre in the black ghetto. Among these tactics are the building-in of apprentice leadership practices in organizations involving younger and newly active members of groups. In addition, a procedure for setting up agreements with other groups, for rotating or staggering specific campaigns, fund drives, and program efforts can be effective. In this way the overtaxed officers of the most effective groups can be available to provide technical assistance and advice to groups in which they could not otherwise be so active. We have also noted in our Detroit research the cooperation between one neighborhood group and another in holding joint meetings, borrowing outside "experts" and using them cooperatively. Similar devices to spread available resources to as many groups as possible are necessary.

Is Local Control the Answer for Ghetto Neighborhoods? The advocates of local control, can draw little comfort from the data collected in our Detroit study. We found that the notion of relying on the local neighborhood, admittedly subject to varying definitions as to size and geographical boundary, can only be marginally effective. Our data show that only under conditions of relative homogeneity can the black neighborhood become a social world with effective bases for integrating the individual and also linking up those activities in the local neighborhood with those of the local black or white community.

But it is precisely the absence of a moderate degree of homogeneity and the existence of artificially homogeneous or excessively heterogeneous neighborhoods that become one of the basic issues concerning black ghetto structure. Thus, the very existence of issues in the local neighborhood which can serve to knit together interests of individuals with diverse status, becomes a problem as to organizational forms by which the area can become a viable decision-making unit.

If we argue that the effectiveness of local control rests in part on the validity of its decisions for the constituents in a given area (representativeness of various structures), then we have evidence from our Detroit study that such local representative government is difficult to create or find in the black ghetto.

The fact that local groups flourish and are active and may be more prevalent in black communities than in white ones is supported in our analysis. This certainly represents one of the major findings. Yet it is not on the issue of the *proliferation* of organizations but in the *effectiveness* with which they function as bases of involving all members of a local neighborhood that their Achilles' heel is to be found.

A major study by Weissman in a black neighborhood in a New York neighborhood produced the following conclusion:

Neighborhood councils are very much in the style of middle-class, Protestant politics . . . in creating new forms of neighborhood integration DuPont did not attempt to integrate the neighborhood around itself. Instead, the council used itself to foster the integration into the neighborhood of other systems such as the schools, politics, and housing. Much of the traditional thinking about councils has implied that a council should become the focal point of neighborhood life, as was the town meeting in the small New England community. The DuPont experience contradicts this emphasis and points the way toward a more delimited use of councils as organizational tools for effecting various neighborhood social systems. . . .

The neighborhood is no more a small town than it is an underdeveloped country. The old DuPont council was successful primarily because it did not try to recreate an organic community. Rather it sought to relate the area to the citywide system.[7]

Weissman's conclusions have particular relevance for our Detroit ghetto findings when we consider the linkage function as a primary goal of local black organizations; we feel this to be one of the critical sources of effective action in the local community. In contrast to viewing neighborhoods as self-contained communities, whose resources and structures may become some kind of miniature city hall, we often ignore the fact that black neighborhoods are far from being "natural" communities.

The role of the local neighborhood organization should not be to define specific functions apart from other social systems. It should be to integrate the newcomer and give him a better chance to participate effectively in the range of institutions which reach and touch that particular neighborhood. It does not serve to supplant or discourage participation in other groups. Effective cross-communication could help resolve the conflicting character of local and nonlocal participation that often places the black ghetto resident in a paradoxical position regarding social change and action.

The role of local organizations in black neighborhoods often differs from that in the typical white neighborhood. Such structures often must seek to be ad hoc in character, to be formed around specific issues, to be able to involve their membership in the important issues of the day, and to "borrow" both resources and personnel from other organizations. Even though this is true of any community which seeks to avoid petrification and rigidity in its organizational patterns, it is particularly important for black groups to eschew the route of setting up structures which then need to justify their own existence.

Instead, the value of organizational patterns must be in the very flexibility of their goals and the looseness of their organizational structure so they can come into and go out of business as the issue demands. This minimizes the potential for splitting energy efforts of leadership between local problems, which may bear little significance in the long run for changes in the black ghetto, and those larger and more distant issues which are often abstract and not relevant to the specific needs of a local black neighborhood.

To emphasize the larger social change issues at the expense of the needs of the local population is merely to perpetuate a pattern of alienation which undermines participation and the sense of worth which comes from involving oneself in any collective effort.

Reevaluating Programmatic Strategies for Social Action in the Black Neighborhood

We have described the connections between neighborhood and voluntary association patterns in the black ghetto. In highlighting the major findings from our Detroit study a critique of several strategies for community action is implied. Many such efforts have grown out of Federal legislation developed during the "Great Society" and "War on Poverty" era. These programs have now begun to come under analysis and scholarly evaluation by persons in the public administration, and the legal and behavioral science disciplines. As a result we have become accustomed to the postmortem assessments of many of these efforts of the 1960s.

Assessing the Community Action Programs (CAP) on the West Coast, Kramer makes this point about programs which were evaluated:

The issues selected by these groups were generally of immediate local concern representing the lowest common denominator or interest and rarely involved the development of any long-range plans. Usually they involved seeking remedial action in a consensual manner rather than through protest or direct action. . . . Most of these neighborhood organizations were quite conventional in their structure, observing formal parliamentary procedure and utilizing agendas and fact-finding consensual models of decision-making similar to those used by middle class improvement associations or councils. Generally they provided opportunities for participation to the more upwardly mobile.[8]

The same author also describes the problems of maintaining member involvement, membership turnover, and the tendency to become pre-occupied with "vested interests" instead of "shared concerns."

Yet all of the accepted problems of CAP, Model Cities programs, or Community Council movements in large urban centers provide only the most nebulous of assaults on such efforts. Descriptions of the neighborhoods and communities in which such programs are analyzed are not systematic, comparable, or clearly focused. We do not know if any of the factors emphasized in our discussion—specifically such considerations as heterogeneity of neighborhood—play a role in the success or failure of these programs.

The present Detroit study has indicated that in heterogeneous black neighborhoods there is a high degree of selective membership, whereas in the black homogeneous neighborhood, there is a strong reliance on the block club and very geographically focused organizations. The effects of selective membership, on the one hand, become dysfunctional only to the extent that a neighborhood is dealing with problems which require going outside of that local sphere. The local organization becomes effective only to the extent that it is able to provide solutions not merely to local problems, but as a representative unit and the primary building block to link the individual through a series of intermediate steps to the larger black or white social structure.

There is reason to question from our Detroit data whether Community Action Agencies (CAA) were failures because they did not achieve their originally stated goal of representing the interests of the poor to governmental structures. The conventional critique of such efforts is summarized in a review discussion of several such efforts by Stewart Perry:

The promise of the CAA was that it would be an instrument that would represent the poor (especially the black poor) and be their advocate in eliciting resources for them from the more affluent environment. The reality was a disappointment. . . . The worst disappointment was that the CAA did not represent the poor; it really represented the whole local community, the rich and middle class as well as the poor.[9]

Perry goes on to ascribe the failure to the fact that "this was in part a result of the composition of the CAA Boards," which had one-third of their members appointed by local government, one-third from social agencies, and only the remaining third selected from local residents. Perry at the same time points out that "a whole new cadre of leaders developed as a result. . . . In this CAAs were successful; by investing in the development of human leadership capital (however unintentionally) they produced a new resource for the poor neighborhoods—a pool of individuals with the social vocabulary of experiences and skills necessary for moving through the system to secure opportunity for their neighborhood."[10]

What Perry has only hinted at may in fact be treated as the specific direction of social policy implied from our Detroit findings. If the commentary about the overly wide representation of CAA boards is taken down to the local neighborhood level, a mechanism particularly suited to the black heterogeneous neighborhood is implied. If, as we have seen, such areas are relatively isolated from the larger black community and the institutions of local government, then any linkage which can be introduced will reduce this parochialism. At the same time, the tendency for existing voluntary associations in such neighborhoods to be selective in membership in order to survive means that they cannot take on the task of serving as a link between the total neighborhood and the larger political system.

The type of heavy involvement from the higher status members of what may be a mixed lower and middle income black area in the CAA type of program can reduce the dichotomy of local-nonlocal involvement we have found in our Detroit research. By creating a suitable forum for fairly wide status groups to participate (as Perry indicates, they do have a tendency to "represent the whole community") the CAP type of structure seems a viable and needed intervention group for black heterogeneous neighborhoods. Nevertheless, its suitability for homogeneous areas is clearly in doubt. In this latter type of black neighborhood the existing groups may well be able to articulate local concerns and to provide, within their own linkages with other non-neighborhood groups and institutions, the kind of advocacy that is needed in local concerns. Introducing another layer of organizational involvement—in effect lengthening the decision-making chain—may serve only to slow down effective action and to lead those in the local neighborhood to perceive the government-sponsored Action group as a means of unwarranted manipulation and control.

In our view, the local government, federally sponsored citizens' action group can work effectively in black ghettoes provided the diagnosis of the neighborhood is carefully developed. It is therefore in the selective use of such programs as CAP and Model Cities, the latter focused on smaller and more meaningful social boundaries of neighborhood, that the greatest effectiveness in community organization will be achieved.

Community Development Corporations: Local Economic Initiatives. A type of community decentralization that takes on certain features of local government is the community corporation. As an outgrowth of the war on poverty, at first these agencies were organized as private nonprofit corporations by neighborhood residents seeking a greater voice in the administration of Community Action Programs. In New York they gained authority to plan and coordinate antipoverty activities in a number of local low income areas; in other municipalities they became service-providing or project-administering organizations under contract with CAP agencies. Model Cities further generated the formation and utilization of these groups. In both Oakland, California, and Dayton, Ohio, corporations were formed as a means of bargaining for resident control over program planning and execution.

Economic objectives are paramount in CDC efforts in contrast to the more direct community development and political action goals of earlier federally stimulated neighborhood programs. Geoffrey Faux, a leading proponent of the concept, defines CDCs as "organizations created and controlled by people living in impoverished areas for the purpose of planning, stimulating, financing and, when necessary, owning and operating businesses that will provide employment, income, and a better life for the residents."[11]

Among the activities commonly engaged in by CDC organizations are job training, owning and managing businesses, providing technical assistance to locality entrepreneurs, and stimulating investments in their neighborhoods. Most of the existing CDCs depend heavily on OEO grants, Model Cities' funds, and Small Business Administration loans to sustain their operations. Kramer, in discussing West Coast CDCs argues that this approach "constitutes the most feasible model whereby low-income residents could acquire a base of power that could effect the quantity and quality of resources available to them."[12] The basic role of such corporations would not be the carving out of highly selective memberships with loyalties to local areas, but instead to "strengthen existing low-income indigenous organizations: social, religious, and civic, by providing them with staff, technical assistance, funds and other resources so that they can operate their own programs and serve another arena, where participation and leadership skills can be developed."[13] Kramer goes on to argue that "neighborhood corporations, which would include such functional associations, could also play an important role in any city-wide coalition."[14]

Commentators on the CDC approach have been critical and indicate that, in general, it has not proven a viable solution to the economic development problems of black ghettoes. As a "corporation based in one geographic area and controlled democratically by the residents," decision-making tends to be stultified by the political goals centered around community control. In an analysis of CDCs, the conclusion was reached that "the objective of creating a 'cohesive' unit in the ghetto through involving a maximum number of people in the decision-making process of the community corporation is one which has proved to be largely impractical."[15] A Harvard Law Review survey states that:

In practice there has been little community-wide participation in all but a very few community corporations. Generally control of the corporation rests in the hands of the leaders who established them. This concentration of control appears to be due in large part to the need to devote almost all energies to establishing a viable business organization, rather than expending efforts to inform, motivate, and organize large numbers of community persons.[16]

In pointing out the apparent failures of the CDC, the Harvard Law Review analysis emphasized the confusion in original goals of CDCs and the incompatibility of social and economic goals. The analysis by Frederick Sturdivant concludes that:

The primary objective must be the establishment of self-sufficient, viable enterprises which are capable of attracting the necessary financial, technical, and managerial resources. In short, many of the broader social service benefits must be viewed as long-range. Shareholders and managers must recognize that if resources are to be attracted and utilized effectively the objective of local control and democratic rule by the area residents must be subordinated.[17]

In discussing the CDC approach, we can directly link the characteristics of homogeneous versus heterogeneous black neighborhoods to the analysis. In several respects the factors we have identified with each of the two ghetto settings suggest conditions under which the

CDC idea is doomed to failure and also when it might be especially viable. In considering the heterogeneous neighborhood we can note how CDC simply does not fit in. Efforts to bridge value differences in the local neighborhood, to link up with external institutions, and to provide efficient decision-making are all seriously impaired in such a neighborhood setting.

As applied to homogeneous black neighborhoods, the CDC concept would appear to offer real promise of success. Since these locales already have some ties to other areas and also need not develop extensive participation by residents to be "representative" of the area, excessive time spent on building consensus is not required. Given the generally similar socioeconomic level of residents, rapid dissemination of ideas and experiences learned by those active in the CDC would be readily utilized by other residents. Effective restriction of actual decision making to an active group within the neighborhood would not be perceived as a "power play" or as a sell-out of other residents as it might be in the heterogeneous neighborhood setting. In addition, in terms of specific economic goals, CDC operations can be concentrated on without producing a breach in trust. In the heterogeneous neighborhood, individual mobility striving and appointment to new organizations often suggest lack of commitment to the total neighborhood. Competitive goal setting and the seeking of optimal approaches to problems is suspect and costly to any organization allowing a high degree of open dissent. By contrast, in the homogeneous neighborhood mobility channels are not dependent on sponsorship by governmental structures like Model Cities, so that a more genuinely indigenous leadership cadre can be developed. Moreover, existing neighborhood leaders and their groups in homogeneous neighborhoods appear to be more effectively interlocked in contrast to heterogeneous black areas.

There is another argument for utilizing the CDC concept selectively in black neighborhoods. Recent trends in corporate management and location theory of business firms have emphasized the cost effectiveness of decentralization. If the trend in private manufacturing and allied business enterprises gathers momentum, then the notion of providing small plants employing a hundred or so workers in local neighborhoods may become more feasible. If the larger corporate firms as well as those growing within the black ghetto can draw upon alternatives of location, which include cosponsorship or stimulation by CDCs, then more might be realized in economic returns from this mechanism than has occurred to date.

Our argument for the appliability of the CDC approach presumes a highly developed and significant neighborhood setting. Our Detroit research indicates that, with the capacity of selected black neighborhoods to draw upon outside expertise and yet to retain the effectiveness and credibility of indigenous formal and informal structures, such an approach should receive support in terms of a range of alternatives from purely private as well as mixed public and private industry efforts.

Dysfunctional Stress on Territoriality

The need to develop the local neighborhood as a springboard for participation in the larger society rather than as a mechanism for heightening the parochial tendencies of local structures has been a major theme of the analysis we have developed. One of the distinctive problems identified in the current study has been the role of the informal leadership structure. Evidence of the greater complexity of social structure in black communities (or, more specifically, the lack of articulation between formal and informal structures of leadership) raises serious questions about the success of increasing the decision-making chain of command in neighborhoods in the ghetto. Moreover, the tendencies for local leadership and organizations to increase isolation, rather than to reduce it, must be addressed by social agencies and efforts involving the local residents.

While the example of artificially created homogeneity of public housing neighborhoods represents a special case of local structure, the broader issue of types of neighborhood contexts is of major concern. The present study points out the diversity of black neighborhoods and suggests the need to treat social organization efforts in light of the complex of status and organizational patterns found within what might otherwise be assumed to be a rather similar set of community contexts.

To the extent that any program of social service delivery, of governmental intervention, or of local self-help generalizes the pattern of organization and the strategy of participation from one local neighborhood to another, there is a high risk of failure. By contrast, to the degree that recognition is accorded to the notion that the local neighborhood is a critical unit but need not be the primary focal base of organization, efforts at social change may be more successful.

The major point we are making is this: *rather than transforming the issue of local neighborhood as central building blocks into an advocacy for local neighborhood programming, we are suggesting that the character of local neighborhood contexts become critical alternatives in the design of social interventions.* This position stands in sharp contrast to the advocates of a uniform "local control" emphasis. Given the diversity of neighborhoods in the black ghetto, policy formulations which seek to neutralize and even to counter the effects of the local neighborhood must also be reconsidered. Unwarranted reliance on local "turf" can limit the use of strategies which emphasize change processes based on reaching persons only peripherally tied to their neighborhood of residence but linked to other community institutions as critical reference groups, that is, bases of personal identification.

As Amitai Etzioni has pointed out in his discussion of the need in contemporary society for "portability" of institutions, their functioning without reference to specific geographical settings, may be the most desirable strategy in the highly interdependent and dynamic patterns which characterize industrialized urban centers. Thus the black ghetto may well have emerged on the urban scene at precisely the time that territoriality per se is no longer a valid or significant basis for individual linkage to "cultures" or community. Nor may the geographical concentration of blacks serve as the power base—except in the most restricted sense of neighborhood succession.

Consequently, it is only in particular types of situations that advocates of neighborhood government may find their case supported. Knowing that the prime issue in urban social change is the capacity to use knowledge to reach power centers, reliance upon a small unit in organizing social action can be a futile, distracting activity. Rainwater, in discussing problems of poverty and discrimination, states that:

The forces that maintain deprivation and exclusion are generally not ones that operate most significantly within the context of the neighborhood or even the community, but ones that operate nationally. Even a highly unified neighborhood action group could probably obtain little for its people from the community power structure; without achieving their goals, they would quickly lose their power even if they could for a short while achieve a solid power base.[18]

Need for Further Concern Beyond Power Shift

Our argument rests on the twin realities of ghettoization as we have elaborated them in our analysis: first, the fact that a differentiated community cannot seek growth and development by a stress upon community cohesion alone. Monolithic solutions to ghetto problems from any direction—internal or external—deny a basic reality: the existence of class conflict and the need to insulate and recognize the diverging interests represented within the ghettoized community. Secondly, from a sociological perspective, black urban ghettoes are structurally complex and require the full expression of such diversity in order that meaningful solutions to the problems confronting black urban dwellers can be developed. For unity in a structural sense there must be a stress upon often differing goals and means. Just as the individual who faces role conflict manifests symptoms of psychological stress, so communities which lack a degree of structural differentiation cannot possibly harness their full resources for change.

Since the end of white paternalism and control is seen as the first and most urgent step in the achievement of black psychological and cultural health, as well as economic justice, it is difficult to argue that policy-makers in the black community should be concerned with what is left to be done once power is transferred. Yet the existence of the ghetto is a continuing social fact. Its unique social structure will persist in the future irrespective of changes in the upper levels of power.

Appendix

Selected Tables from Survey Analysis

TABLE 1A

Correlation Ratios for "Vertical" and "Nonvertical" Status Effects

Race	*Black*	*White*
Proportion of variation in anomie explained by:		
Vertical (social class effects)		
Income	1.55%	1.54%
Education	3.47	4.17
Occupation	1.38	5.89
Combined main effects	6.40	11.60
Nonvertical (inconsistency effects)		
All interaction effects	18.07	5.13
Total	24.47%	16.73%

Finding: The variation in attitudes of anomie is affected by status inconsistency more among blacks than is the case for whites in the survey sample in Detroit.

TABLE 2A

Neighborhood Status Inconsistency and Organizational Participation

	Status consistent		*Moderately inconsistent*		*Sharply inconsistent*	
	Black	White	Black	White	Black	White
See neighbors in all organizations	27.7%	21.3%	31.2%	18.3%	31.2%	20.1%
See neighbors at some organizations	22.4	24.0	22.3	36.7	32.5	27.4
Do not see neighbors at organizations	19.1	22.7	14.0	29.6	19.5	29.4
Do not belong to organizations	30.8	32.2	32.5	15.4	16.9	23.2
Total	100.0%	100.2%	100.0%	100.0%	100.1%	100.1%
N =	470	409	314	196	144	159

Finding: Blacks who have a status different from their neighbors are more likely than whites to belong to organizations where neighbors are always members, while whites who are status inconsistent are more likely than blacks in the same situation to belong to groups where neighbors are not members.

TABLE 3A

Effects of Types of Status Inconsistency on Local Community Participation

		Status consistent	*Status inconsistent: neighborhood norms*	*Status inconsistent: community norms*	*Status inconsistent on both*
Percentage of members of block clubs or neighborhood associations who report being active in the group	Black	40.5%+	12.6%−	40.8%+	16.9%−
	White	35.6	30.8	36.2	45.2 +
Ratio of church members who see neighbors versus those who do not	Black	1.8:1	1.0:1−	2.3:1+	1.6:1
	White	2.2:1	2.2:1	2.4:1	2.1:1

Finding: The effects of status inconsistency on activism in block clubs and neighborhood associations are greater for blacks than whites, with neighborhood inconsistency sharply reducing participation. With regard to church membership, a similar pattern occurs in the extent of contact with neighbors.

TABLE 4A

Distribution of Black and White Neighborhoods High on Each of the Functions of Neighborhood

	Black	*White*
Social context/reference group	56.3%* (9/16)	16.7% (2/12)
Interaction arena	56.3* (9/16)	16.7 (2/12)
Interpersonal influence	50.0 (8/16)	8.3 (1/12)
Status arena	43.4 (7/16)	50.0 (6/12)
Mutual aid	37.5 (6/16)	41.7 (5/12)
Organizational base	31.3 (5/16)	33.3 (4/12)
Mean rank for all six indices	50.0%* (8/16)	16.7% (2/12)

*Race difference statistically significant at .05 level or beyond, direction or prediction.

Finding: Black neighborhoods are significantly higher than white areas on 3 out of 6 functions of neighborhoods. Using an overall average of functions, black areas are twice as likely to be above the mean compared to white areas.

TABLE 5A

Distribution of Neighborhood Types Derived from Detroit Area Sample of 28 Locales

	Black	*White*	*Total*	
Integral................	2	1	3	10.7%
Parochial	3+	1	4	14.3
Diffuse	3	2	5	17.9
	8+	4−		
Stepping-stone...........	3	4+	7	25.0
Transitory	1	1	2	7.1
Anomic................	4	3	7	25.0
	8	8		
Total................	16	12	28	100.0%

Finding: Black neighborhoods are more likely to be among those types reflecting a strong reference group tie to the local area as opposed to those which are reflective of weak orientations to the neighborhood.

TABLE 6A

Neighborhood Utilization of Formal and Informal Service Delivery Systems

	Percentage of respondents using at least one community service[a] (Formal) (A)	*Percentage of respondents using more than 5 (mean) neighbor service[b] (Informal) (B)*	*Emphasis on Formal service structure (A − B)*	*Total service utilization (A + B)*
Integral.........	58.7% ←——→	55.7%	+ 3.0%	114.4%
Parochial	39.5 ——→	57.9	− 18.4	97.4
Diffuse	39.1 ——→	54.1	− 15.0	93.2
Stepping-stone...	54.1 ←—→	48.8	+ 5.3	102.9
Transitory	52.3 ←——	36.8	+ 15.5	89.1
Anomic.........	47.2 ←——→	45.6	+ 1.6	92.8

[a] The median was use of one or more services which include: (1) health clinic, (2) community center or settlement house, (3) welfare department, (4) ADC, (5) family service agency, (6) Salvation Army, (7) police, (8) guidance or youth service clinic, (9) employment service, (10) visiting nurse services.
[b] Neighbor aid includes: (1) keeping an eye on young children playing, (2) taking a child while on vacation, (3) helping someone who is sick, (4) keeping an eye on a house if the occupant is away for a month, (5) doing something about a school principal not doing a good job, (6) organizing protest against some city action, (7) borrowing a few dollars temporarily.

Finding: Neighborhoods use formal and informal systems differently, some are best at using formal only or informal only, others use both.

TABLE 7A

**Distribution of Neighborhoods by Race and Number of
Qualifying Modal Patterns of Socioeconomic Status***

	Black		*White*	
No qualifying modes	6	37.5%↰	2	16.7%↰
One qualifying mode	5	31.3	4	33.3
Two qualifying modes	5	31.3	3	25.0
Three qualifying modes	0	0.0 ↲	3	25.0 ↲
Total	16	100.1%	12	100.0%

*Qualifying modes refer to the criteria established for income, education, and occupation clustering in each neighborhood. Where diversity on each of the factors resulted in too small a percentage of persons with similar attributes (the modal criteria) that neighborhood was "disqualified" for homogeneity.

Finding: Black neighborhoods cluster at the extreme of heterogeneity whereas white neighborhoods show a wide distribution with regard to the same variable.

TABLE 8A

Heterogeneity and Homogeneity of Suburban Versus Central City Neighborhoods

	Central City		*Suburban*	
	Black	*White*	*Black*	*White*
Heterogeneous	75.0%	62.5%	50.0%	25.0%
Homogeneous	25.0	37.5	50.0	75.0
Total	100.0%	100.0%	100.0%	100.0%
	(N=12)	(N=08)	(N=04)	(N=04)

Finding: Neighborhoods most likely to be heterogeneous are black inner city ones; those most likely to be homogeneous are white suburban ones.

TABLE 9A

Neighborhood as Reference Group in Relation to Neighborhood Type

Heterogeneous		*Homogeneous*	
Black 47.0%	White 47.8%	Black 59.3%	White 48.0%
(N = 640)	(N = 370)	(N = 270)	(N = 369)

Finding: Blacks living in homogeneous neighborhoods are more likely than other respondents to have a highly positive reference orientation to their local areas of residence.

TABLE 10A

Respondent-Called City Agencies in Relation to Neighborhood Type

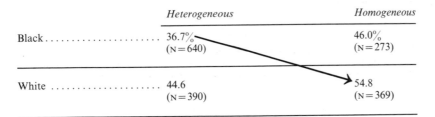

	Heterogeneous	*Homogeneous*
Black	36.7% (N = 640)	46.0% (N = 273)
White	44.6 (N = 390)	54.8 (N = 369)

Finding: Blacks living in heterogeneous neighborhoods are least likely to contact city agencies, while whites living in homogeneous areas are most likely to make such contacts.

TABLE 11A

Participation Patterns in Relation to Neighborhood Type

	Heterogeneous		Homogeneous	
	Black	White	Black	White
Exclusive pattern (see neighbors at all organizations or do not see neighbors)	47.1%	44.2%	45.8%	48.0%
Mixed pattern (sometimes see neighbors, sometimes not see neighbors in organizations)	20.9	22.4	31.9	31.8
Respondent does not belong to any organizations	32.0	33.4	22.3	20.2
Total	100.0%	100.0%	100.0%	100.0%
Ratio of exclusive to mixed patterns of participation	2.25:1	1.97:1	1.44:1	1.51:1

Finding: Blacks in heterogeneous neighborhoods are more likely than persons in other settings to have an exclusively in or out of neighborhood pattern of organizational participation than to have a mixed pattern of group memberships.

TABLE 12A

Group Functions Index Score in Relation To Race and Neighborhood Type

*Number of reported group functions**	Heterogeneous		Homogeneous	
	Black	White	Black	White
6–7	28.1%+	16.7%	34.1%+	20.8%
1–5	37.2	44.7	42.2	53.7
0.	34.5	38.6	23.8	25.6
Not ascertained	0.2	0.0	0.0	0.0
Total	100.0%	100.0%	100.1%	100.1%

*In response to the question: "Have the groups you belong to provided you with any of the following kinds of experiences?" seven specific items were included: (1) making new friends, (2) learning about city government and the community, (3) learning how to improve own economic position, (4) meeting people who have helped improve job or general economic situation, (5) coming in contact with new ideas and ways of thinking, (6) giving a chance to express own skills and talents that are not used in work, and (7) meeting people who are in a better class of the community.

Finding: Regardless of neighborhood setting, blacks use organizations in a greater variety of ways than do whites. At the same time persons in homogeneous settings use organizations for more functions than those residing in heterogeneous neighborhoods. This is particularly true for black respondents in the study.

TABLE 13A

Black Consciousness Scale* in Relation to Organizational Participation

	Black
See neighbors in all organizations	48.7%
Mixed—see neighbors in some organizations	57.1%
Do not see neighbors at organizations	49.4%
Respondent does not belong to organizations	39.8%

*The black consciousness scale is based upon responses to the following eight questions—whether the person "mainly agrees", "mainly disagrees" or has "no definite feeling": (1) Civil rights groups which have white and black leaders would be better off without whites, (2) whenever possible a person should buy from a black owned store, (3) blacks should not have anything to do with whites if they can help it, (4) if economic conditions were not an issue, I would prefer to live in a separate black nation, (5) being black is more than skin color—it's a state of mind, (6) white people cannot possibly understand what it is to be black, (7) black people are brighter than white people—that is how they have survived, and (8) white society offers nothing but corruption and false values to blacks.

Finding: Blacks who belong to voluntary organizations are more likely to have above average black consciousness. In particular where a person is a member of some groups where neighbors belong and some where they do not, black consciousness is most likely to be above the median level.

TABLE 14A

Leader Interviews by Type of Organization in Black and White Neighborhoods

	Black	*White*
Block club	43.0%	9.9%
PTA	22.0	25.7
Church group	11.0	13.9
Veterans' group	0.0	4.0
Fraternal group	3.0	3.0
National group	0.0	3.0
Professional group	1.0	3.0
Youth group	0.0	3.0
Labor union	6.0	9.9
Social club	0.0	1.0
Political party club	2.0	4.0
Civil rights group	2.0	1.0
Political or social action group	1.0	1.0
Business or civic group	7.0	13.9
Senior citizens' group	1.0	1.0
Study, cultural groups	1.0	3.0
Total	100.0%	100.3%
	(N = 100)	(N = 101)

Finding: Block clubs are far more common in the sample of black organization leaders, while business, labor, and other non-neighborhood groups are more common for white organization leaders.

TABLE 15A

**Membership Size Reported by Organization Leaders by
Race and Neighborhood Type**

	Black		White	
	Hetero-geneous	*Homo-geneous*	*Hetero-geneous*	*Homo-geneous*
1–25 people............	39.3%	33.3%	13.9%	15.1%
26–50 people............	23.0	24.2	2.8	7.5
51–99 people............	18.0	12.1	13.9	32.1
100 or more people.......	19.7−	30.4	69.4+	45.3
Total................	100.0%	100.0%	100.0%	100.0%
	(n=64)	(n=36)	(n=45)	(n=56)

Finding: In general, groups sampled in heterogeneous neighborhoods tend to be smaller in size than those found in homogeneous areas. Black heterogeneous settings are least likely to have groups of large size while comparable white areas are most likely to have memberships of 100 or more.

TABLE 16A

**Leader-Reported Change in Organizational Participation by
Race and Neighborhood Type**

	Black		White	
	Hetero-geneous	*Homo-geneous*	*Hetero-geneous*	*Homo-geneous*
More members have joined than left group	33.3%	55.6%	26.2%	29.6%
Number of members has remained the same in last year	42.9	22.2	45.2	44.4
Number of members remained the same but a lot of turnover.................	6.3	11.1	14.3	11.1
More members have left than joined in last year.........................	15.9	8.3	14.3	14.8
Don't know, not ascertained.....	1.6	2.8	0.0	0.0
Total......................	100.0%	100.0%	100.0%	99.9%

Finding: Black organizations sampled in homogeneous neighborhoods are more likely than other groups to report membership increase in the recent past.

TABLE 17A

**Leader-Respondent Report of Why Persons are Chosen as
Organizational Leaders, by Race and Neighborhood Type**

	Black		White	
	Hetero-geneous	Homo-geneous	Hetero-geneous	Homo-geneous
Because they have good ideas and programs	23.8%	50.0%	34.9%	42.9%
Views reflect the thinking of the majority of the group	34.9	22.2	27.9	30.4
Because they have past experience in organizations	27.0	19.4	20.9	16.1
Because of their education and social standing	11.1	5.6	2.3	3.6
Other, not ascertained	3.2	2.8	14.0	7.0
Total......................	100.0%	100.0%	100.0%	100.0%

Finding: For both blacks and whites, leaders of groups chosen in homogeneous compared to heterogeneous neighborhoods are selected for their innovativeness. Particularly in black heterogeneous neighborhood settings group leaders are chosen for their conformity to majority opinion and past experience—a conservative leadership pattern.

TABLE 18A

Incremental Goal Displacement

Leader-Respondent Report of Shift in Goals and Handling of Internal Diversity by Perceived Status Conflict in the Organization

	Black		*White*	
	High status conflict	*Low status conflict*	*High status conflict*	*Low status conflict*
Things true of group: when people disagree at meetings they usually have a good reason for doing so	65.9%	78.6%	70.6%	80.6%
True of group: people using the group to promote their point of view—"doing their own thing" versus working on the problem at hand	31.8	8.9	17.6	14.9
True of group: trying to handle too many different issues	22.7	5.4	26.5+	10.4
True of group: too much time spent keeping people in agreement instead of going ahead with the needed programs	22.7	5.4	14.7	10.4

Finding: Black organizations with high internal status conflict show the highest level of irrelevant or distracting group process compared to other organizations.

TABLE 19A

**Leader-Respondent Report of Where Members of
Organizations Live, by Race and Neighborhood Type**

| | Black | | White | |
	Hetero-geneous	Homo-geneous	Hetero-geneous	Homo-geneous
All live in neighborhood	55.0%	55.6%	52.5%	39.3%
Most live in neighborhood	25.0	8.3	17.5	14.3
Half live in neighborhood	10.0	22.2	12.5	17.9
Most live out of neighborhood	10.0	13.9	17.5	28.6
Total......................	100.0%	100.0%	100.0%	100.1%
	(N=64)	(N=36)	(N=40)	(N=56)

Finding: Black organizations in heterogeneous or homogeneous settings are similar in having a majority where only neighbors belong. Black groups in heterogeneous areas are the least likely of all settings to contain persons who are residents beyond the local neighborhood.

TABLE 20A

**Leader-Respondent Report of Members of Organization
Active Outside the Neighborhood by Race and Neighborhood Type**

| | Black | | White | |
	Hetero-geneous	Homo-geneous	Hetero-geneous	Homo-geneous
75% or more active.............	11.1%	54.5%	21.9%	53.7%
50–75% active	20.7	12.1	37.5	26.8
Less than 50% active	68.2	33.4	40.6	19.4
Total......................	100.0%	100.0%	100.0%	99.9%
	(N=64)	(N=36)	(N=45)	(N=56)

Finding: Organizations located in heterogeneous neighborhoods are more likely than other groups to have most of their members not active in groups outside of the local area. Organizations in black heterogeneous neighborhoods are distinct in having most of their members with no outside-neighborhood group activity.

TABLE 21A

**Neighborhood Type and Race in Relation to Naming of an
Activist in Central City and Suburban Neighborhoods**
(percentage knowing of an activist)

	Black		*White*	
	Heterogeneous	*Homogeneous*	*Heterogeneous*	*Homogeneous*
Central city neighborhoods ..	29.2% −	39.0%	30.5% −	38.1%
Suburban neighborhoods ..	28.2 −	23.0 −	60.7 +	51.8+

Finding: Blacks in homogeneous central city neighborhoods and whites in heterogeneous suburban settings are most likely to know of a neighborhood activist. While whites in suburbs of all types know activists more than whites in central city neighborhoods, this pattern does not prevail for blacks.

TABLE 22A

**Coalescence of Nominations of Neighborhood Activists in
Relation to Neighborhood Type and Race**

10 percent or more of nominations of the same activists

	Heterogeneous neighborhoods		*Homogeneous neighborhoods*	
Black......................	3/11	27.2%	3/5	60.0%
White	1/6	16.7	4/6	66.7
Total....................	4/17	23.6%	7/11	63.5%

Finding: Homogeneous neighborhoods are significantly more likely to have persons naming the same person as a neighborhood activist than is the case in heterogeneous settings. Differences in this regard are narrower between homogeneous and heterogeneous black neighborhoods.

TABLE 23A

Neighborhood Type and Race in Relation to
Activists Who Know Other Neighborhood Activists
(percentage knowing of an activist)

	Heterogeneous	*Homogeneous*
Black	46.5%	66.7%
White	62.5	67.5

Finding: Black heterogeneous neighborhoods show the lowest pattern of all settings in terms of neighborhood activists being a tight-knit group.

TABLE 24A

Neighborhood Type and Race in Relation to
Activist Person Being an Officer of a Voluntary Association

	Heterogeneous	*Homogeneous*
Black	63.1%	81.0%
White	84.0	90.5

Finding: Black heterogeneous neighborhoods are lowest in comparison with other settings in terms of formal and informal leadership linkage.

TABLE 25A

Neighborhood Type and Race in Relation to Officers in
Voluntary Associations Being Neighborhood Activists

	Heterogeneous	*Homogeneous*
Black	18.7%	16.5%
White	44.2	27.0

Finding: White heterogeneous neighborhoods are more likely than other settings to "coopt" informal leadership; black homogeneous are least likely.

TABLE 26A

Rate of Completed Interviews in Relation to
Listed Addresses of Original Sample
(includes activists)

	Black	White
Completed interview	69.9%	70.3%
No contact–not at home (two call-backs)	11.2	9.8
No contact– address vacant	3.0	1.5
No contact–other reasons or not specified by interviewer	4.0	0.6
Contact–interview not completed–refusal	11.8	17.7
Total	99.9%	99.9%
	(N = 1387)	(N = 1081)

TABLE 27A

Rate of Completed Interviews Where Contact with
Potential Respondent Was Made
(includes activists)

	Black	White
Completed interview	82.3%	79.8%
Completed interview, wrong race[a]	3.4	0.1
Explicit refusal	9.9	15.0
Failed to keep appointment	1.2	1.6
Other reasons[b]	3.4	3.5
Total	100.2%	100.0%
	(N = 1134)	(N = 952)

[a] This means neighborhood race designation as black or white in original drawing of sample.
[b] Includes interview breakoffs, invalid interviews, respondent on vacation, ill, etc.

TABLE 28A

Sample Characteristics: Employment Status of Respondent

	Black	*White*
Employed	58.7%	56.2%
Unemployed	7.4	3.3
Housewife	16.3	25.6
Retired	14.7	13.3
Student	0.7	0.5
Not ascertained	2.0	0.9
Total	99.8%	99.8%
	(N = 864)	(N = 632)

TABLE 29A

Sample Characteristics: Education of Respondent

	Black	*White*
0–8 grades	31.3%	22.8%
9–11 grades	25.9	19.2
High school graduate	27.1	31.6
1–2 years college	8.2	11.6
3–4 years college	3.9	8.7
Graduate or professional school	3.0	4.3
Not ascertained	0.5	1.6
Total	99.9%	99.8%

TABLE 30A

Sample Characteristics: Income of Family of Respondent in 1968

	Black	*White*
Under $2,000	5.2%	4.6%
$2,000–4,999	17.8	13.4
$5,000–7,999	19.4	13.3
$8,000–9,999	19.0	16.0
$10,000–14,999	23.5	35.5
$15,000 or more	5.7	12.7
Not ascertained	9.2	4.3
Total	99.8%	99.8%

Notes

Introduction

1. Perhaps the most widely discussed instance of social research becoming the focus of such attention is the so-called Moynihan Report. This analysis of black family demographic trends shows that 25% of black families are headed by females. This became the basis for describing the alleged disintegration of family life and the pattern of matriarchical hegemony. See Daniel P. Moynihan, *The Negro Family: The Case for National Action* (Washington, D.C.: U.S. Department of Labor, Office of Planning and Research, March 1965). The controversy which swirled around this report is fully explored in Lee Rainwater and William L. Yancey, *The Moynihan Report and the Politics of Controversy* (Cambridge, Massachusetts: M.I.T. Press, 1967).
2. Whitney M. Young Jr., "Studying a Sick Society." Syndicated article in the *Michigan Chronicle* (March 30, 1968).
3. Martin Luther King, Jr., "The Role of the Behavioral Scientist in the Civil Rights Movement." *The American Psychologist*, XXIII, 3 (March 1968), p. 180.
4. Ibid.
5. Ibid.
6. Stanley H. Smith, "The Institutional Setting of the Sociological Contributions of Black Sociologists: A Case Study." Paper presented at the Conference of Black Sociologists: Historical and Contemporary Perspectives, University of Chicago, May 1972.
7. Wilson Record, "White Sociologists and Black Studies." Paper presented at the Annual Meeting of the American Sociological Association, New Orleans, Louisiana, August 1972, pp. 3–4.
8. Ibid., p. 1.
9. This is true with respect to the decades of the 1950s and 1960s following earlier work by a number of black and white sociologists. The only recent empirical study is an analysis of black organizational participation in Tampa's black community, entitled *Black Belonging* (Westport, Conn.: Greenwood Publishing, 1971). The authors, Jack C. Ross and Raymond H. Wheeler, utilized three survey samples to test hypotheses about the relationship between work and participation in community associations. This study is an exception to the numerous survey comparisons of blacks

and whites in which aggregations of respondents are compared. In the Tampa studies the specific object of analysis was a black community and its organizational patterns, not a set of samples of blacks in different cities.

10.   The survey studies were carried out in the spring and summer of 1969. The research was sponsored by the National Institute of Mental Health (Grant # 1 R01-16403). Extensive efforts at local neighborhood "participant observation" data were also collected as part of the overall study. Black and white students from the University of Michigan along with professionally trained interviewers from Detroit served as the field staff for the research.

Interviews with black and white respondents began in March of 1969 and continued through the month of July 1969. During this period a total of 1692 persons were contacted and completed interviews. Of this number 1496 were selected from a random listing of dwelling-unit addresses in 28 elementary school districts in Detroit, Inkster, and River Rouge, Michigan. An additional neighborhood in Dearborn, Michigan was also included in the study. The map (page 22) indicates the geographical boundaries and location of each neighborhood.

The sampling procedure used in this survey is a combination of purposive and cluster sampling designs. The purposive basis for the selection of respondents is based upon a comparison of racially homogeneous local areas. Cluster sampling was employed once the neighborhood unit was defined, with a 5% sample of addresses used as the initial population. Neighborhoods were chosen by first employing the figures on racial composition of elementary schools in the city of Detroit. Those school districts which were either 95% or more black, or 95% or more white, were retained as potential neighborhoods. From the original 197 elementary school districts a total of 66 qualified as all black and 35 fitted criteria for an all-white area. The remaining 96 schools were not included in the next stage of sampling.

The final stage in the sampling process involved the selection of an eligible respondent in the sample dwelling unit. Interviewers were instructed to contact the married or unmarried head of household, 21 years of age or older. It was decided that interviewers would "call back" two times in the event a potential survey participant failed to keep the interview appointment. By this procedure 864 black and 632 whites were able to complete an interview. Added to this group were 196 persons who are "neighborhood activists" (see chapter 6). A separate "leader" survey provided 201 interviews beyond those already indicated. Thus a total of 1893 interviews were obtained as part of the overall study. In the Appendix (tables 29 through 34) various characteristics of the base sample are described.

Chapter I

1.   Gunnar Myrdal, *An American Dilemma* (New York: Harper and Row, 1944), p. 928.

2.   Ibid., p. 952.

3. Ibid., p. 954.
4. E. Franklin Frazier, *Black Bourgeoisie* (Glencoe, Illinois: Free Press, 1957), p. 162.
5. Ibid., p. 178.
6. Nathan Hare, *The Black Anglo-Saxons* (New York: Macmillan, 1970), pp. 33–34.
7. Floyd Hunter, *Community Power Structure* (Chapel Hill: University of North Carolina Press, 1953).
8. C. Wright Mills, *The Power Elite* (New York: Oxford Press, 1956).
9. Hunter, op. cit., pp. 114, 168.
10. Andrew Billingsley, *Black Families in White America* (Englewood Cliffs, N.J.: Prentice-Hall, 1968), p. 122.
11. St. Clair Drake, "The Social and Economic Status of the Negro in the United States," *Daedalus*, XCIV, 4 (Fall 1965), p. 785.
12. G. Franklin Edwards, "Community and Class Realities: The Ordeal of Change," *Daedalus*, XCV, 1 (Winter 1966), p. 16.
13. Jessie Bernard, *Marriage and Family Among Negroes* (Englewood Cliffs, N.J.: Prentice-Hall, 1966).
14. Billingsley, op. cit., p. 123.
15. Nathan Glazer, "Blacks and Ethnic Groups: The Difference and the Political Difference it Makes," *Social Problems*, XVIII (Spring 1971), pp. 459–60.
16. Edwin Harwood, "Urbanism as a Way of Negro Life," chapter 1 in *Life Styles in the Black Ghetto* by William McCord, John Howard, Bernard Friedberg and Edwin Harwood (New York: W. W. Norton & Company, 1969), p. 21.
17. Ibid., pp. 28–30.
18. Norbert Wiley, "The Ethnic Mobility Trap," *Social Problems*, XV (Winter 1971), pp. 147–59.
19. For a discussion of the "solo" versus the firm lawyer, see Jack Ladinsky, "Careers of Lawyers, Law Practice, and Legal Institutions," *American Sociological Review*, XXVIII (February 1963), pp. 47–54.
20. Amitai Etzioni, "The Ghetto—A Re-evaluation," *Social Forces*, XXXVII (March 1959), p. 258.
21. Ibid., p. 257.
22. A discussion of six stages in ethnic group assimilation is also contained in Andrew M. Greeley, *Why Can't They Be Like Us?* (New York: E.P. Dutton & Company, 1971).
23. Robert Blauner, "Internal Colonialism and Ghetto Revolt," *Social Problems*, XVI (Spring 1969), p. 397.
24. William K. Tabb, "Race Relations Models and Social Change," *Social Problems*, XVIII (Spring 1971), p. 438.
25. Ibid., p. 435.
26. Ibid., p. 442.

Chapter II

1. In fact, however, it is more accurate to say that less publicity was given nationally to this high-rise public housing area of 430,000 residents—98%

of whom are black. The Brooklyn New York enclave of blacks did have what has been termed "minor disturbances" on July 29, 1967, during the week of Detroit's "urban disorder." Twenty-seven arrests took place and in subsequent days minor street destruction continued. For a commentary and analysis of community organization in the Bedford-Stuyvesant area by two white sociologist-actionists, see Henry Etzkowitz and Gerald Schflander, *Ghetto Crisis: Bureaucracy vs. Progress in Bedford-Stuyvesant*, (Boston: Little, Brown & Company, 1969). A 1964 disturbance in the same locale is discussed by J. R. Feagin, "Social Sources of Support for Violence in a Negro Ghetto," *Social Problems*, XV (Spring 1968), pp. 432–41.

2. For valuable discussion comparing three major social psychological theories of who riots, see Nathan M. Kaplan and Jeffrey M. Paige, "A Study of Ghetto Rioters," *Scientific American*, CCXIX (August 1968), pp. 15–21. Another valuable comparison of theories is the paper by Allan D. Grimshaw, "Civil Disturbance, Racial Revolt, Class Assault: Three Views of Urban Violence," paper presented at the American Sociological Association, New York, August 1967. A more recent attempt to examine the Watts, Los Angeles, disturbance using a model of epidemic diffusion is the work by Margaret Abudu, Walter Raine, Stephen Burbeck and Keith Davison, "Black Ghetto Violence: A Case Study Inquiry into the Spatial Pattern of Four Los Angeles Riot Event-Types," *Social Problems*, XIX (Winter 1972), pp. 408–27.

3. The Model Cities area includes a part of the West Side Twelfth Street area of rioting but is centered largely *between* the East and West Side disturbance areas. As such the Model Cities neighborhood has a higher concentration of low income both black and white residents than the "civil disorder" neighborhoods.

4. The author has made the argument that those local neighborhoods which were centers of riot activity were not the most anomic settings of the black ghetto. See Donald I. Warren, "Neighborhood Structure and Riot Behavior in Detroit: Some Exploratory Findings," *Social Problems*, XVI (Spring 1969), pp. 464–84.

5. This approach is exemplified in the work of Robert Park, R. D. MacKenzie, and later in the development of work by their students. See, for example, Amos H. Hawley *Human Ecology* (New York: Ronald Press Co., 1950); James A. Quinn, *Human Ecology* (New York: Prentice-Hall, 1950).

6. This perspective is developed in Otis D. Duncan and Leo F. Schnore "Cultural, Behavioral, and Ecological Perspectives in the Study of Social Organization," *American Journal of Sociology*, LXV (September 1959), pp. 132–46. See also Leo F. Schnore, "The Myth of Human Ecology," *Sociological Inquiry*, XXXI, 2 (1961), pp. 128–49.

7. Durkheim applied the notion of a distinct level of "social facts" to the suicides within a society: "instead of seeing in them only separate occurrences unrelated and to be separately studied, the suicides committed in a given society during a given period of time are taken as a whole, it

appears that this total is not simply a sum of independent units . . . but is itself a new fact sui generis with its own unity, individuality and consequently its own nature." *Suicide*, translated by John A. Spaulding and George Simpson (New York: Free Press, 1951), p. 46.

8.   St. Clair Drake and Horace R. Cayton, *Black Metropolis* (New York: Harper Torchbook, 1962), p. 12.

9.   Harold M. Rose describes the black ghetto in the following terms:

> It is the aggregate of census tracts which . . . conforms to the neighborhood scale. Thus it is a series of contiguous neighborhoods which might be described as the ghetto spatial configuration. When the population within a given census tract equals or exceeds 50% black, then that tract will be said to constitute a ghetto neighborhood. Ghetto core neighborhoods are represented by census tracts whose population is 75% or more black, with ghetto fringe neighborhoods having 50 to 74% of their population identified as black. [*The Black Ghetto* (New York: McGraw-Hill, 1971), p. 5.]

10. Mason Haire, "Biological Models and Empirical Histories of the Growth of Organizations" in Mason Haire (ed.), *Modern Organization Theory* (New York: John Wiley & Sons Inc., 1959), pp. 287–93.

11. The report of this methodology is contained in Ralph V. Smith, Stanley E. Flory, and Rashid L. Bashshur, *Community Interaction and Racial Integration in the Detroit Area: An Ecological Analysis*, Eastern Michigan University, Project #2557, U.S. Office of Education (September 8, 1967).

12. This concept is discussed in Kenneth E. Boulding, "Toward a General Theory of Growth," *Canadian Journal of Economic and Political Science* (August 1953), pp. 326–40.

13. See on this point Arthur J. Vidich and Joseph Bensman, *Small Town in Mass Society* (Princeton, N.J.: Princeton University Press, 1958).

14. Robert S. Lynd and Helen M. Lynd, *Middletown* (New York: Harcourt, Brace and Company, 1929). This pioneering empirical study of a community was followed by a later examination of the same community entitled *Middleton in Transition* (same publisher, 1937).

15. For example see W. Lloyd Warner, *Democracy in Jonesville* (New York: Harper and Row, 1949).

16. Karl E. Taeuber and Alma F. Taeuber, *Negroes in Cities* (Chicago: Aldine Publishing Company, 1965), p. 182.

17. Wilfred Marston investigated the hypothesis that black communities are less decentralized and that this is related to differentiation within the black community. His specific hypothesis is that "the Negro community is a miniature urban complex characterized by the decentralization of those higher in social status in a pattern analogous to that found in the urban white community." Eighteen cities ranging in size from 100,000 to 1,000,000 were included in the study. He further observes that:

> For the Negro community, the central city-suburban distinction of the total urban complex indicated that expansion of the Negro community is often not outward. The newer somewhat higher prestige Negro residential neighborhoods are frequently located as close to the city

center as are the older somewhat lower prestige Negro residential neighborhoods. In fact, in some cases, emerging area segments are actually closer to the city center. [Wilfred G. Marston, "Population Redistribution and Socio-Economic Differentiation Within Negro Areas of American Cities." Paper presented at the 62nd Annual Meeting of the American Sociological Association, San Francisco, California (August 1967), p. 5.]

18. Eugene S. Uyeki, "Residential Distribution and Stratification, 1950– 1960," *American Journal of Sociology*, LXVI (March 1964), pp. 490–98. Uyeki found that whites had greater occupational differentiation in Cleveland and Chicago and that this pattern remained unchanged from 1950 to 1960.

19. Hortense Powdermaker, *After Freedom* (New York: Viking, 1939), p. 13.

20. Andrew Billingsley, *Black Families in White America* (Englewood Cliffs, N.J.: Prentice-Hall, 1968), p. 124.

21. Robert C. Weaver, *The Negro Ghetto* (New York: Harcourt, Brace & Company, 1947), p. 211.

22. Williams presents the issue in the following manner:

The thesis of this work is that social class indices, as they are commonly employed in sociological research, are not useful in analyzing Negro attitudinal and behavioral data. Current social class indices are constructed on the basis of social stratification configurations characteristic of the white community. The particular and unique conditions of the Negro community are unaccounted for by these indices. By applying these indices to Negroes found in samples of predominantly white populations, the researcher ignores a significant social variable—the differential stratification systems of the white and Negro communities. [Jay R. Williams, *Social Stratification and the Negro American: An Exploration of Some Problems in Social Class Measurement*, doctoral dissertation, Duke University, 1969, p. 2.]

23. Kenneth B. Clark, *Dark Ghetto* (New York: Harper and Row, 1965), p. 196.

24. Louis A. Ferman and Patricia R. Ferman, *The Irregular Economy*, unpublished manuscript, Institute of Labor & Industrial Relations, University of Michigan, 1973.

25. For an analysis of the relation of source of information about this police-community crisis see Donald I. Warren "Mass Media and Racial Crisis: A Study of the New Bethel Church Incident in Detroit," *Journal of Social Issues*, XXVIII, 1 (1972), pp. 111–32.

26. Donald R. Deskins, Jr., "Interaction Patterns and the Spatial Form of the Ghetto," Special Publications No. 3, Department of Geography, Northwestern University, Evanston, Ill.

Chapter III

1. See Daniel P. Moynihan, *The Negro Family: The Case For National Action* (Washington, D.C.: U.S. Department of Labor, Office of Planning and Research, March 1965).

2. Daniel C. Thompson, "An Approach to the Black Experience." Paper

read at the 67th Annual Meeting of the American Sociological Association, (August 1972), p. 5.

3. This term is derived from the now classic polemic of E. Franklin Frazier, *Black Bourgeoisie* (Glencoe, Illinois: Free Press, 1957).

4. Nathan Hare, *Black Anglo-Saxons* (New York: Macmillan, 1970). The work of both Hare and Frazier offers criticism of middle class blacks, especially in terms of the emulation of white life styles and participation patterns.

5. While this term has been employed in a variety of studies and social class treatises, a discussion especially pertinent to the black context is that of Lee Rainwater, "The Crucible of Identity: The Negro Lower-Class Family," *Daedalus*, XCV, 1 (Winter 1966), pp. 172–216.

6. See, for example, August B. Hollingshead, *Elmtown's Youth* (New York: John Wiley & Sons, 1949).

7. The so-called "Yankee City" series contains the basic work which Warner carried in the tradition of community stratification studies. W. Lloyd Warner and Paul S. Lunt, *The Social Life of a Modern Community*, vols. I and II (Ithaca, New York: Yale University Press, 1941, 1942).

8. Jay Williams, *Social Stratification and the Negro American: An Exploration of some Problems in Social Class Measurement*, doctoral dissertation, Duke University, 1969. Several instances are cited here in which major studies of social stratification have treated blacks as a group requiring distinct analysis. The effect of this strategy often means that less than adequate attention has been given to black stratification. At least one text on social class does not even refer to "Negro" in its index. See Leonard Reissman, *Class in American Society* (Glencoe, Illinois: The Free Press), 1959.

9. St. Clair Drake and Horace R. Cayton, *Black Metropolis* (New York: Harper Torchbook, 1962), p. 521. The authors go on to state that "Class-thinking is essentially a way of sizing up individuals in terms of whether they are social equals, fit for acceptance as friends, as intimate associates, and as marriage partners for one's self or one's children."

10. Drake and Cayton, op. cit., p. 782.

11. Williams concludes that:

> In reality, little is known about the Negro stratification system. Researchers who may be interested in this area of study will of necessity have to "start from scratch". . . . The best predictors to patterns of behavior will be perceptions and attitudes rather than income, occupation, and other demographic variables (Williams, op. cit., p. 140).

12. Ibid., p. 139.

13. An experience of the author underscores the issue of perceived social distance in the black ghetto. While walking with a sociology undergraduate student—a senior at the time—a ten-year-old passed him on the sidewalk with the greeting: "hello there, Doctor Brown. How are you today?" In other words the fact of a person being identified in their own local neighborhood as attending college was enough to create a large gap in social prestige.

14.   Nathan Glazer and Daniel P. Moynihan, *Beyond the Melting Pot* (Cambridge, Mass.: M.I.T. Press, 1963), p. 64.

15.   There has been a wide range of studies which have used this concept to analyze individual attitudes and behavior. The progenitor of recent interest in the effects of differing rank positions on multiple status indicators is the work of Gerhard Lenski. See, for example, "Status Crystalization: A Non-Vertical Dimension of Status," *American Sociological Review*, XIX (August 1954), pp. 405–12; "Social Participation and Status Crystallization," *American Sociological Review*, XXI (April 1956), pp. 458–66. For a review of the concept of status inconsistency-incongruence see Andrej Malewski "The Degree of Status Incongruence and Its Effects," in Reinhard Bendix and Seymour M. Lipset (eds.), *Class, Status and Power*, 2 ed., (New York: Free Press, 1966). For an application of the concept to black rioters, see Donald I. Warren, "Neighborhood Status Modality and Riot Behavior: An Analysis of the Detroit Disorders of 1967," *Sociological Inquiry* (Summer 1971), pp. 350–68. For important discussion of methodological and theoretical issues regarding status inconsistency analysis, see Donald R. Ploch, *Status Inconsistency: A Method of Measurement and Evaluation*, unpublished dissertation, University of North Carolina, Chapel Hill, North Carolina, 1968.

16.   Because some researchers have found little effect in their research from the status inconsistency factor, the value of this concept has been subject to criticism. One virtually ignored aspect of the issue is that often the socioeconomic rankings of a person along with their religio-ethnic position are together used to evaluate inconsistency effects. The argument we have developed and applied in the current Detroit study is to look within an ethnic community and show the effects of inconsistency on "achieved" dimensions of status and therefore, in effect to hold constant the "ascribed" ranking of status. In doing this we can show that even if socioeconomic rankings may not universally produce important inconsistency effects for all populations—perhaps not especially for whites—their effects for various minority and ethnic groups can serve as an important element of influence, in addition to vertical social class levels themselves.

Chapter IV

1.   See, for example, Robert E. Park, "The City: Suggestions for the Investigation of Human Behavior in the City Environment," *American Journal of Sociology*, X (1915), pp. 577–612; *Human Communities* (Glencoe, Illinois: Free Press, 1952); R. D. McKenzie, "Demography, Human Geography and Human Ecology," in L. L. Bernard, *The Field and Methods of Sociology* (New York: Luig and Smith, 1934). A classic study of the mental health patterns of different zones of the city is that by Robert E. L. Faris and H. Warren Dunham, *Mental Disorders in Urban Areas* (Chicago: University of Chicago Press, 1939).

2.   The issue of using a spatial definition of community is one which has been debated frequently in the sociological literature. See, for example, Christen T. Jonassen, "Community Typology," in M. B. Sussman (ed.), *Community*

Structure and Analysis (New York: Crowell, 1959), pp. 16–36. Also see Arnold S. Feldman and Charles Tilly, "The Interaction of Social and Physical Space," *American Sociological Review*, XXV (December 1960), pp. 877–84. Recent research on community has centered on the notion of "social networks" and the functions which such nonspatially defined "reference groups" play in the life of individuals.

3. Peter H. Mann, "The Socially Balanced Neighborhood Unit," *Town Planning Review*, XXVIII (July 1958), pp. 91–98.

4. This concept is closely associated with the human ecology approach and is exemplified in the work of Eshref Shevsky. See E. Shevsky and W. Bell, *Social Area Analysis* (Stanford: Stanford University Press, 1955).

5. Marvin B. Sussman (ed.), *Community Structure and Analysis* (New York: Crowell), 1959, pp. 61–92.

6. Herbert Gans, *The Urban Villagers* (New York: Free Press), 1962.

7. Gerald D. Suttles, *The Social Order of the Slum* (Chicago: University of Chicago Press, 1968).

8. See for example Eugene Litwak and Philip Fellin, "Neighborhood Cohesion under Conditions of Mobility," *American Sociological Review* XXVIII (June 1963), pp. 364–76.

9. Theodore Caplow and Robert Forman, "Neighborhood Interaction in a Homogeneous Community," *American Sociological Review* XV (June 1950), pp. 357–66.

10. Judith T. Shuval, "The Micro-Neighborhood: An Approach to Ecological Patterns of Ethnic Groups," *Social Problems* IX (Winter 1962), pp. 272–80.

11. Shimon E. Spiro, *Effects of Neighborhood Characteristics on Participation in Voluntary Associations*, doctoral dissertation, University of Michigan, 1968.

12. Scott Greer, "Urbanism Reconsidered: A Comparative Study of Local Areas in a Metropolis," *American Sociological Review* XXI (February 1956), pp. 19–25.

13. Eugene Litwak and Ivan Szelenyi, "Primary Group Structures and Their Functions: Kin, Neighbors, and Friends," *American Sociological Review*, XXXIV (August 1969), pp. 465–81.

14. See Elihu Katz, "The Two-Step Flow of Communication: An Up-to-Date Report on an Hypothesis," *Public Opinion Quarterly*, XXI (Spring 1957), pp. 61–78. Earlier discussion of "opinion leaders" is contained in Paul F. Lazarsfeld, Bernard Berelson, and Hazel Gaudet, *The People's Choice* (New York: Columbia University Press, 1948).

15. See William H. Form and Sigmund Nosow, *Community Disaster* (New York: Harper and Row, 1958).

16. Louis Kriesberg and Seymour S. Bellin, *Fatherless Families and Housing: A Study of Dependency*, Final Report, U.S. Department of Health, Education and Welfare, Welfare Administration, 1965.

17. See, for example, Alan B. Wilson, "Residential Segregation of Social Classes and Aspirations of High School Boys," *American Sociological Review*, XXIV (December 1959), pp. 836–45; William H. Sewell and

Michael J. Armer, "Neighborhood Context and College Plans," *American Sociological Review*, XXXI (April 1966), pp. 159–68.

18. See Wilson, op cit.
19. See Sewell and Armer, op. cit.
20. This concept of "pluralistic ignorance."
21. Litwak and Fellin, op. cit., p. 369.
22. Robert C. Angell, "The Moral Integration of American Cities," *American Journal of Sociology*, LVII (July 1952).
23. Suzanne Keller, *The Urban Neighborhood: A Sociological Perspective* (New York: Random House, 1968).
24. Philip Fellin and Eugene Litwak, "The Neighborhood in Urban Society," *Social Work*, XIII (July 1968), p. 75.
25. Suttles, op. cit., p. 123.
26. In the Detroit research neighborhoods were classified as to heterogeneity using a multidimensional approach. The samples of respondents from each of the 28 areas were measured in terms of level of family income, education of respondent, and occupation of head of household. Using definitions of the modal pattern on each variable, a neighborhood could have from zero to three "qualifying modes," depending on how clustered the respondents interviewed were. Neighborhoods were called "heterogeneous" in the analysis if they had zero or only one qualifying mode, while those areas with two or three modal socioeconomic clusterings were defined as "homogeneous." If income alone is used, the result shows that black areas are more likely to be either very heterogeneous or very homogeneous. The method used throughout most of the study—three dimensions of status—results in black neighborhoods being skewed heavily in the heterogeneous direction vis-à-vis white areas. In addition, black neighborhoods which qualified as heterogeneous tend to fall in the transitory and anomic categories. By contrast fewer black heterogeneous areas are either integral, parochial or diffuse. See Appendix, table 10.

Chapter V

1. Among the more inclusive summaries along these lines are the following: Murray Hausknecht, *The Joiners* (New York: Bedminster Press, 1962); Shimon Ernst Spiro, "Effects of Neighborhood Characteristics on Participation in Voluntary Associations," unpublished dissertation, University of Michigan, 1968, pp. 6–29; and Charles R. Wright and Herbert H. Hyman, "Voluntary Association Membership of American Adults: Evidence from National Sample Surveys," *American Sociological Review*, XXIII (June 1958), pp. 284–94. Robert W. Hodge and Donald J. Treiman, "Social Participation and Social Status," *American Sociological Review*, XXXIII (October 1968), p. 728; and W. Lloyd Warner and James C. Abegglen, *Big Business Leaders in America* (New York: Atheneum, 1963), pp. 152 ff.
2. See Wright and Hyman, op. cit.
3. Anthony Orum, "A Reappraisal of the Social and Political Participation of Negroes," *American Journal of Sociology*, LXXII (July 1966), pp. 32–46;

Nicholas Babchuk and Ralph V. Thompson, "Voluntary Associations of Negroes," *American Sociological Review*, XXVII (October 1962), pp. 647–55; Wright and Hyman, op. cit.

4. See Judith R. Kramer, *The American Minority Community* (New York: Thomas Y. Crowell, 1970).
5. Gunnar Myrdal, *An American Dilemma* (New York: Harper and Row, 1944), p. 954.
6. See Orum, op. cit., p. 45.
7. E. Franklin Frazier, *Black Bourgeoisie* (Glencoe, Illinois: Free Press, 1957).
8. Nathan Hare, *Black Anglo-Saxons* (New York: Macmillan, 1970).
9. An additional reason advanced for low participation of blacks in voluntary associations is the fear related to white intimidation, particularly in Southern cities. A documentation of this is presented in J. C. Ross and R. Wheeler, "Structural Sources of Threat to Negro Membership in Militant Voluntary Associations in a Southern City," *Social Forces*, XLV (June 1966), pp. 583–86.
10. Orum, op. cit. p. 45.
11. More recent analysis of replicated national sample surveys shows a general increase in voluntary association participation by all groups, but especially blacks. See Herbert H. Hyman and Charles C. Wright, "Trends in Voluntary Association Memberships of American Adults: Replication Based on Secondary Analysis of National Sample Surveys," *American Sociological Review*, XXVI (April, 1971), pp. 191–206.
12. Marvin Olsen, "Social and Political Participation of Blacks," *American Sociological Review*, XXXV (August 1970).
13. Ibid., p. 684.
14. Ibid., p. 696.
15. This discussion of functional roles of organizations relies heavily on the discussion by Gist and Fava. They list the following functions: (1) confer status or power; (2) provide a mechanism for the socialization of members in with prevailing values or ideologies; (3) reference groups to marshall public opinion; (4) provide a sense of security for the individual because in conformity there is comfort and in union there is strength, real or fancied; (5) fellowship, escape from routine; (6) a ladder for upward or downward mobility; (7) bolster status quo through exclusion of outsiders; (8) dissemination of information and ideas; (9) link individual with the outer world. See Noel P. Gist and Sylvia F. Fava, *Urban Society*, 5 ed., (New York: Crowell, 1964), p. 385 f. The points of particular relevance to our argument include (1), (2), (4), (6), and (9).
16. See Scott Greer and Peter Orleans, "Mass Society and Parapolitical Structure," *American Sociological Review*, XXVII (October 1962), p. 645.
17. Another way to consider the relationship between social status level and voluntary association memberships is to correlate the number of such memberships with the status level. Thus a positive correlation would show that as one's status goes up, so does the number of organizational affiliations. Using correlation coefficients, we can then say how much participation level is related to status position. In the Detroit data we find

that little difference exists for blacks and whites and that for both groups education is most highly related to number of memberships.

At the same time, for the number of groups in which neighbors are members, income level and occupation show more than twice the correlation (+0.22 to +0.11 and +0.27 to +0.12) for blacks compared to whites. In other words, participation with neighbors is more significantly tied to status level for blacks than for whites. Putting the matter another way, our data show that belonging to groups where neighbors are participants is a phenomenon which increases with status. By contrast, whites of high status are not more likely to be involved with neighbor-linked organizations than are low status whites. Thus for the black ghetto "localism" in participation is not the critical factor. If there is a problem of unity derived from the social mobility of middle class blacks, drawing them away from community participation, it is not a question of neighborhood involvement per se, but of the quality and character of local groups and their functions.

18.   To this extent then, we need to talk about the high degree of participation which occurs among blacks who are either high or low status, using socioeconomic measures.

In addition we find among blacks, using an index of "black consciousness" or ethnic identity, that there is a higher proportion of persons with that identity among those who belong to at least one voluntary association. This tends to correspond with the earlier findings of Olsen that, when there are norms of participation in the ethnic community, those who identify most closely with that ethnic community are more likely to conform to its norms. In this case it means a greater level of participation in voluntary organizations (see Appendix, table 13A).

19.   These additional interviews were completely separate from the original survey conducted with all respondents in the sample. Often this meant that the same individual was contacted twice: once in the capacity of a randomly selected member of the selected neighborhoods and a second time if they indicated on the first interview that they held an office in a voluntary association. Consequently the "leader" interview is linked to the original survey but contains entirely different questions. "Officers" are the base of the sample, not residents, and a sampling from this universe formed the basis of the second survey effort. As respondents these "leaders" become "key informants" about their organizations. Thus the main content of the interview served as a kind of indirect "observational" approach to what "participant observation" of a more extensive and direct form might accomplish.

20.   The work on the functional content of groups using these concepts can be traced to the following sources: R. Freed Bales, *Interaction Process Analysis: A Method for the Study of Small Groups* (Reading, Mass.: Addison-Wesley, 1950); R. Freed Bales, "Task and Social Roles in Problem-Solving Groups" in Eleanor Maccoby, T. M. Newcomb, and E. L. Hartley (eds.), *Readings in Social Psychology*, 3 ed. (New York: Holt, Rinehart and Winston, 1958); R. F. Bales and P. E. Slater, "Role

Differentiation in Small Decision-Making Groups," in Talcott Parsons and R. Freed Bales (eds.), *Family, Socialization and Interaction Process* (Glencoe, Illinois: Free Press, 1955).

21. Thus the cadre of professional caseworkers, special education teachers, school officials, and welfare agency or antipoverty program staff professionals are the trained experts focusing on the social problems of the ghetto. As an ascendant status group they may be compared to the middle management, accounting, and rising young lawyers who serve corporations in the white community. One by-product of creating the "social problem professionals" of the black ghetto is that channels of upward mobility are opened which tend to reduce the pressure on the more traditional white professions and industrial hierarchies to admit blacks to their ranks. This process of providing "functional alternatives" for individuals in the black ghetto has, of course, other analogues in the less prestigious spheres of organized crime and blue-collar employment. While some might argue this view, such patterns are a special form of institutional racism in which blacks are advanced as specialists in the sphere of black life and problems. Such a process might be more valuable for the black ghetto if it were not apparent that the institutional structures of American urban society are highly centralized in terms of power and control, and the creation of adjunct or parallel structures only serves to overspecialize and fragment the energies of black professionals and those with college training.

22. One might argue that there is a spill-over effect—organizations found in homogeneous neighborhoods may have a very high portion of their members who come from other areas. But the evidence does support this kind of dynamic. See Appendix, table 19A.

23. A special index was constructed to measure the internal status conflict level of a voluntary association. This consisted of a series of 18 different interview items focusing on the extent of reported differences due to education, income, or occupation caused problems. The median point on the index provided a dichotomization of organizations into "high" and "low" status conflict.

24. The specific wording used in the interview form was: "people using the group to promote their own point of view"; "too much time spent on keeping people in agreement instead of moving ahead with needed programs"; "people of different backgrounds not getting along together" (see Appendix, table 18A).

Chapter VI

1. Floyd Hunter, *Community Power Structure* (Chapel Hill: University of North Carolina Press, 1953). There are extensive critical reactions to the approach used by Hunter. For an excellent collection of articles on the concepts and methodology in community power studies see Willis D. Hawley and Frederick M. Wirt, *The Search for Community Power* (Englewood Cliffs, N.J.: Prentice-Hall, 1968). Our discussion of the "neighborhood activist" is different from that of Hunter and others who sought to

define the "top leadership" in a community. Moreover the closure of leadership using mutually named leaders is only superficially employed in our analysis.

2.   The survey design for neighborhood activists involved drawing up a list of persons named when the cross-section interviewing was completed in a given neighborhood. When the final total of nominees was known, the fraction of one-half was utilized as the selection criterion. Names were randomly selected and the potential activist contacted. The interview content matched that of other respondents but additional supplemental questions on strategies of activism were also included. The completion rate reflects losses due to outright refusals, break-off of interviews, ineligible by virtue of illness and incorrect or erroneous information. In this latter category were instances of incorrect addresses where new information was not available as well as misspelled or mispronounced names which could not be traced further. No effort was made to recontact a respondent who gave incomplete or inaccurate information. In the event that a previously interviewed respondent turned out to be a nominated activist—this occurred in 5 cases—then only the supplement was completed with the second interview visit.

Utilizing the procedure we have discussed, 79.9% of the white and 76.5% of the black neighborhood activists completed interviews. The resulting sample includes 81 black and 115 white respondents.

3.   Recent work on the flow of information across homogeneous groups stresses the role of a bridging person who links each and provides a "weak tie." See Mark S. Granovetter, "The Strength of Weak Ties," *American Journal of Sociology* LXXVIII (May 1973), pp. 1360–80, and Robert W. Duff and William T. Liu, "The Strength in Weak Ties," *Public Opinion Quarterly* 36 (Fall 1972), pp. 361–66.

4.   At the same time we find that males are less likely to be officers of voluntary associations in the black community than they are to be nonofficers. A somewhat reverse trend is true in the white community. In other words, what we have seen (which is extremely crucial in terms of the patterns of the black community) is that the informal neighborhood activist is more likely to be a male, but the formal organization officer is more likely to be a female. In the white sample in Detroit we found the reverse to be the case—more often, the neighborhood activist was a female and the organization officer was a male. To this extent we have a mirror image between black and white communities in the role of various kinds of leadership. Certainly one of the significances of this is the fact that stereotypes of the black community as female-dominated do not apply to our data. Instead, the evidence from Detroit shows that sex differences in community roles are important and the black community is distinct in terms of what types of leadership roles are associated with particular sexes, but the pattern is one of differentiation not domination.

5.   This pattern is not present for the sample of white organizational officers and activists. Since, in the black neighborhoods "activists" are the group least likely to be status inconsistent from their neighborhood and officers are somewhat more likely than average to be status inconsistent in this

manner, we have a kind of trade-off of leadership roles. Informal leaders tend to be especially representative of their neighbors; officers are not very representative. This is the black ghetto pattern and is not replicated in the white areas sampled.

If we take only officers of organizations which are neighborhood focused, we find a further differentiation: blacks with status inconsistencies relative to the total sample of blacks tend to be officers of groups with a largely local focus, whereas those who are status inconsistent using the reference point of the local neighborhood are most likely to be officers in groups which do not contain neighbors. No similar "exchange" of participation arenas occurs for the comparable types of white status inconsistents who are officers in voluntary associations. All of which further underscores the special dynamics linking types of status dilemmas of blacks to their arena of social participation.

6. See Eugene Litwak and Henry J. Meyer, "A Balance Theory of Coordination Between Bureaucratic Organizations and Community Primary Groups," *Administrative Science Quarterly*, XI (June 1966), pp. 31–58. In the conceptualization presented by the authors, the extent of "social distance" between a local community group and a formal organization is defined by the types of linkages which are established between the two units. Where a formal organization is in conflict with a local neighborhood in terms of goals or values any mechanism which brings that organization closer will help bridge the gap. But if the local neighborhood has too ready an access to a formal organization, this can deflect the goals of the structure and some insulation is required to prevent this. Thus "outreach" is not uniformly a good thing for an organization since the vitality of local and large-scale groups depends on each being able to function effectively in its own sphere.

7. Marvin E. Olsen, "A Model of Political Participation Strata." Paper read at the 67th Annual Meeting of the American Sociological Association, New Orleans, Louisiana, August 1972.

Chapter VII

1. A recent discussion by Alfred McClung Lee refers to the popularity of the concept:

> As with other fashionably controversial catchwords in social discussions, "alienation" during its current vogue sprouted a variety of meanings. None of them is too precise, but each appears to many to explain a great deal. These meanings are of two types: one includes the more psychological elaborations and projections of Marx's worker alienated from his labor and product. The other stresses social structure, the estrangement of society from its members [Alfred McClung Lee, "An Obituary for 'Alienation,'" *Social Problems*, XX (Summer 1972), pp. 121–22].

Seeman has attempted to define a set of separate dimensions each of which embodies concepts relating to alienation. He defines "Powerlessness," "Meaninglessness," "Normlessness," "Isolation," and "Self-estrangement" as a paradigm not only to bring clarity but also to "work toward a useful conception of each of these meanings." See Melvin Seeman, "On the Meaning of Alienation," *American Sociological Review*, XXIV (24 December 1959), pp. 783–91.

In his subsequent work with the multiple dimensions of alienation Seeman has turned more to the connection that Lee has called the psychological versus social structural levels of analysis. For example, see Melvin Seeman, "Alienation and Social Learning in a Reformatory," *American Journal of Sociology*, LXIX (November 1963), pp. 270–84; also "Alienation and Knowledge-Seeking: A Note on Attitude and Action," *Social Problems*, XX (Summer 1972), pp. 3–17. In this latter discussion and research report Seeman states:

> The most important conclusion is perhaps the most general one that these outcomes inspire. I refer to the demonstration that the alienated *attitudes* with which we have been concerned are not divorced from *actions* of considerable potential importance . . ." [p. 16].

In seeing alienation in a multidimensional way and in action as well as attitude, Seeman opens the concept of alienation in ways which previous writers and social analysts failed to do. As he states: "the sundry alienations which are so prominent in the literature do not constitute a unitary 'package,' and often enough do not work in the packaged way that our dismal theories about them suggest" [Ibid., p. 15].

2.   William A. Gamson, *Power and Discontent* (Homewood, Illinois: Dorsey Press, 1968), p. 42.
3.   Ibid.
4.   Ibid., p. 46.
5.   Ibid., p. 48.
6.   John R. Forward and Jay R. Williams, "Internal-External Control and Black Militancy," *Journal of Social Issues*, XXVI, 1(1970), p. 88.
7.   Ibid.
8.   Jeffery M. Paige, "Political Orientation and Riot Participation," *American Sociological Review*, XXXVI (October 1971), p. 819.
9.   Ibid., p. 811.
10. Ibid.
11. Ibid.
12. For a strongly polemical discussion of such "building" strategies see Henry Etzkowitz and Gerald M. Schaflander, *Ghetto Crisis* (Boston: Little, Brown and Company, 1969).

Chapter VIII

1.   For a valuable critique of the "underdevelopment" concept of black ghetto economics, see Frances F. Piven, "Community Control: Beyond the Rhetoric," *New Generation*, L (Fall 1968), pp. 7–10.
2.   See for example Howard W. Hallman, *Neighborhood Control of Public Programs: Case Studies of Community Corporations and Neighborhood Boards* (New York: Praeger Publishers, 1970). The discussion of a Mobilization for Youth effort in New York has special relevance for other black communities. See George Brager and Harry Specht, "Mobilizing the Poor for Social Action," chapter 14 in Ralph M. Kramer and Harry

Specht (eds.), *Readings in Community Organization Practice* (Englewood Cliffs, N.J.: Prentice-Hall Inc., 1969), pp. 223–32; also John Strange, "A Whole Lot of Protest—and What Do You Get?" in Virginia B. Ermer and John H. Strange (eds.), *Blacks and Bureaucracy* (New York: Crowell, 1972); also P. R. Laurence, "Organizational Development in the Black Ghetto" in R. S. Rosenbloom and R. Marris (eds.), *Social Innovation in the City* (Cambridge, Mass.: Harvard University Press, 1969).

3. On the problem of unclear goals see David Austin, *Resident Participation, Political Mobilization or Organizational Cooperation?* (Florence Heller Graduate School for Advanced Studies in Social Welfare, May, 1970); Robert Hagedorn and Sanford Labovitz, "Participation in Community Associations by Occupation: A Test of Three Theories," *American Sociological Review*, XXXIII (April 1968), pp. 767–83; also William W. Hamilton, "The Cities vs. the People: Citizen Participation in Model Cities," *Everyman's Guide to Federal Programs Impact*, I, 2 (Washington, D.C.: New Community Press, 1969); Daniel P. Moynihan, *Maximum Feasible Misunderstanding* (New York: Free Press, 1969); Irving Lazar, "Which Citizens to Participate in What?" in Cahn and Passett (eds.), *Citizen Participation: A Case Book in Democracy* (New York: Praeger Publishers, 1969).

4. On this point see Albert J. Reiss, Jr. and Howard E. Aldrich, "Absentee Ownership and Management in the Black Ghetto: Social and Economic Consequences," *Social Problems*, XVIII (Winter 1971), pp. 319–39.

5. Piven, op. cit., p. 8.

6. Frederick D. Sturdivant, "Community Development Corporation: The Problem of Mixed Objectives," *Law and Contemporary Problems*, XXXVI (Winter 1971), p. 46.

7. Harold H. Weissman, *Community Councils and Community Control* (Pittsburgh: University of Pittsburgh Press, 1970), pp. 174–75.

8. Ralph H. Kramer, *Participation of the Poor* (Englewood Cliffs, N.J.: Prentice-Hall, 1969), pp. 228–29.

9. Stewart E. Perry, "National Policy and the Community Development Corporation," *Law and Contemporary Problems*, XXXVI (Winter 1971), p. 298.

10. Ibid., p. 299.

11. Geoffrey Faux, *CDC's: New Hope for the Inner City* (New York: Twentieth Century Fund, 1971), p. 29.

12. Kramer, op. cit., p. 270.

13. Ibid., p. 271.

14. Ibid.

15. Sturdivant, op. cit., p. 46.

16. Nels J. Ackerson and Lawrence H. Sharf, "Community Development Corporations: Operations and Financing," *Harvard Law Review*, LXXXIII (1970), p. 1582.

17. Sturdivant, op. cit., p. 49.

18. Lee Rainwater, "Neighborhood Action and Lower-Class Life Style," in John B. Turner (ed.), *Neighborhood Organization for Community Action* (New York: National Association of Social Work, 1968), p. 35.

Glossary

ALIENATION. A widely employed concept in the social sciences with multiple historical roots and contemporary definitions. Used without further specification, we mean to denote individual attitudes generally expressing feelings of isolation, lack of significance, estrangement, and a low level of participation in the social and political processes of the community. *See also* STRUCTURAL ALIENATION, STRUCTURAL ISOLATION.

ANOMIC NEIGHBORHOOD. A local neighborhood/community in which little active participation occurs, where mutual identification among individuals is low, and where a sense of lack of goals, individual or collective, is present.

AUTONOMOUS NEIGHBORHOOD LEADERSHIP. The social structure of a local/neighborhood community in which those who are leaders in organizations are separate from individuals who are identified as active by a cross-section of the population. *See also* FORMAL LEADERSHIP, INFORMAL LEADERSHIP, NEIGHBORHOOD ACTIVIST, OPINION LEADER, SOCIAL STRATIFICATION.

COMPENSATION THEORY. The view, advanced by some researchers, emphasizes the intense "joining" pattern of black Americans as a result of their exclusion from majority white associations. *See also* ISOMORPHISM MODEL OF THE BLACK GHETTO.

CO-OPTATION NEIGHBORHOOD LEADERSHIP. The social structure of a local neighborhood/community where individuals who are identified as active by a cross-section of the population are the same people as those who run local organizations.

CROSS-FERTILIZATION NEIGHBORHOOD LEADERSHIP. The social structure of a local neighborhood/community where the rank and file members of local organizations provide the cadre of active people identified by a cross-section of the population.

DIFFUSE NEIGHBORHOOD. An identified local area in which people who may have moved in at a similar time have similar attributes, such as income or attitudes, but whose contact with one another is rather limited at the individual and collective level.

ECOLOGICAL ANALYSIS. An approach to neighborhoods or communities in which the overall patterns of income, attitude, or behavior are compared—such as the percentage of crime—but where variations within each area are not taken into account. This is opposite to or in contrast to psychological measures of individual differences.

ELITE INTEGRATION NEIGHBORHOOD LEADERSHIP. A local neighborhood/community social structure involving a balance between heads of organizations who also have reputations as active people according to a cross-section of opinions and activists who know about although are not themselves part of the leadership of organizations. Influence and exchange is concentrated at the top of this social structure.

EMULATION THEORY. *See* ISOMORPHISM MODEL OF THE BLACK GHETTO.

EXPRESSIVE LEADERSHIP. This refers to the social-psychological concept, based on small group experiments, in which the leader is a person who can bind people together and who through symbols or actions appeals to the emotional solidarity of the group. "Expressive" goals of a group are those which embody these activities. The term "social-emotional" leadership or integrative goals are other ways in which the same meaning is described in behavioral science literature.

FORMAL LEADERSHIP. A term referring to the individuals who hold offices, elective or appointive in various kinds of organizations of a community. This is in contrast to those who are leaders by reputation rather than having any particular role or specific position. *See also* INFORMAL LEADERSHIP.

FUNCTION. We use this term in relation to its teleological meaning: the role a given part has in relation to other elements. "Social function" means the relationship of some activity or organization to the rest of society or to the individuals involved. The function is imputed rather than self-consciously denoted by the people in the situation. For example, one function of neighborhoods is to give help to people when a sudden illness occurs or if a child is in trouble.

GHETTO, GHETTOIZATION. We use these terms in specific ways to refer both to a territorially demarcated area having a common or predominant social group make-up and to the ways in which this pattern is developed, sustained, and reinforced. *See also* SOCIAL COMPRESSION.

GOAL DISPLACEMENT. A term drawn from the behavioral science literature on large-scale organizations and bureaucracies. It refers to the gradual, often unrecognized change in purposes from those originally professed or officially proclaimed by an organization. It also means the discrepancy between actual behaviors of the people in the organization in contrast to the intended outcomes of their efforts.

GRASS-ROOTS OUTREACH NEIGHBORHOOD LEADERSHIP. The social structure of a local neighborhood/community in which individuals identified as active by a cross-section of the population come to hold positions of leadership in organizations.

HETEROGENEITY. A term used to describe the population characteristics of a neighborhood, organization, or other social group which is based on the high degree of individual differences found within it. *See also* STATUS, STATUS CONFLICT, SOCIAL DIFFERENTIATION, SOCIAL COMPRESSION.

HOMOGENEITY. A term used to describe the population characteristics of a neighborhood, organization, or other social group which is based upon the high degree of similarity in socioeconomic and other individual attributes. *See also* STATUS, STATUS CONFLICT, SOCIAL DIFFERENTIATION, SOCIAL COMPRESSION.

HUMAN ECOLOGY. An approach within the behavioral sciences, and particularly sociology, which stresses the analogy of plant and animal interdependency with the natural environment. In social terms—often described as "social ecology"—analysis of human communities is based on the essential shape and spatial distribution of major living-sustaining activities. As such, human ecology stresses the spatial-temporal patterning and organization of key functions (economic, political, familial) and tends to see subjective values and attitudes as an outgrowth of these processes.

INDIRECT INTERLOCK NEIGHBORHOOD LEADERSHIP. The social structure of a local neighborhood/community based on the awareness of organization members and leaders of a group of active people whose reputation for leadership is derived from the views of a cross-section of people living in that area. Thus formal and informal leadership is linked, not because the same people are playing different roles, but simply by mutual awareness.

INFORMAL LEADERSHIP. A range of community roles based on perceived influence, activism, knowledge, or expertise but which is not located in a formal organization or within a given stratum of the population. *See also* NEIGHBORHOOD ACTIVIST.

INSTITUTIONALIZATION. A general behavioral science concept derived from sociology which refers to the solidifying, regularizing or making permanent of human behavior patterns. It often implies locating a given set of repeated behaviors within a given organization, legal structure, or formalized apparatus specifically established for that purpose. Thus the hospital provides the setting for institutionalizing the role of physician, nurse, patient, or mental illness treatment. Block clubs may institutionalize concern over neighborhood upkeep.

INSTITUTIONAL RACISM. A recently coined but frequently invoked term dealing with the institutionalized effects of individual prejudice. Often this concept is employed to distinguish between those forms of racism which occur irrespective of the attitudes of individuals involved. In this sense institutional racism means the process of maintaining discrimination through given institutional patterns of the society.

INSTRUMENTAL LEADERSHIP. This refers to the social-psychological concept of the roles of individuals in group settings where the survival of the group depends on achieving specific goals, solving given problems before the group.

The actions of leaders or others which stress concrete solutions, press for implementation of given steps, or provide ways to implement desired ends. This is in contrast with "expressive" leadership. Another term used for instrumental individuals are "task leaders." *See also* "EXPRESSIVE" LEADERSHIP, INFORMAL LEADERSHIP.

INTEGRAL NEIGHBORHOOD. An identified local area in which people have a high degree of solidarity, are in contact with one another a great deal, but are also active outside their own local setting. Loyalty to the local area does not conflict with identification with a larger world of participation and values.

INTERORGANIZATIONAL LINKAGE. A term used to describe the existence of contact, knowledge, and exchange of resources between different groups or formal agencies. Referrals, common memberships, and shared meetings are some of the ways in which such ties are manifested.

ISOMORPHISM MODEL OF THE BLACK GHETTO. A term used to characterize the view that black populations have essentially no social structural patterns distinct from other urban groups. In particular, we have used this idea in relation to the social class and neighborhood patterns of black compared to other urban populations.

LEADERSHIP DISPLACEMENT. A term used to describe the process whereby individuals living in a given locale are underrepresented in local groups and who participate more outside of their area of residence than within it. This concept is applied to black neighborhoods and is hypothesized to be more extensive in such settings.

LOCAL NEIGHBORHOOD. A term used to denote the primary sampling unit of our study: the elementary school district. It also may be closely tied with the idea of "a walking distance" neighborhood. It contrasts with the "micro-neighborhood—neighbors living in direct view or at adjacent dwelling units—and the notion of a naturally bounded community area or a census tract statistical unit.

MARGINAL. A concept with several historical roots in sociology and referring to the status of being in two social worlds at once. It generally means the position of never being totally part of any community or social ranking. *See also* STATUS INCONSISTENCY, LEADERSHIP DISPLACEMENT.

MASS SOCIETY THEORY. A set of hypotheses and concepts derived from sociological theorizing in which the individual is seen in relation to two other levels of society: top level elites and intermediate groups and organizations. In this model organizations such as unions or community associations are seen as powerful and vital forces which bring the message of the common man or woman to the attention of the top leaders of the society. In turn, these same organizations buffer the leaders from direct assault by a quixotic and demagogically manipulated "mass" that can destroy representative democracy. In this view the trends and processes of modern societies depend on a balance of the various forces. The viability of local units of community becomes essential in a proper distribution of power that spells the difference between totalitarian control and viable pluralistic democracy.

MAXIMUM FEASIBLE PARTICIPATION. A term derived from the legislative program of the 1960s War on Poverty programs. In particular, it refers to the Model Cities programs and the assumption that poor and black areas of cities had no cohesive or viable neighborhood structures and that poverty was as much a matter of powerlessness as a lack of services.

MUTUAL AID. This refers to the ways in which individuals living in a given neighborhood/community provide services to one another which are not formally organized or specifically required. Often the extent and character of that help is defined by the proximity of neighbors, the emergency character of the problem, or the regular but limited resource sharing that may go on in a local setting. Help may be material, emotional, or informational in form.

NATURAL AREAS. A term used by many sociologists, and particularly the "Chicago School" of human ecologists, to define the special functional character of a neighborhood. Data gathered to define such areas are predominantly census and demographic in character and use the approach of "ecological analysis." The term "social area analysis" was used to describe this approach in the 1940s. *See also* HUMAN ECOLOGY, ECOLOGICAL ANALYSIS.

NEIGHBORHOOD ACTIVIST. A term used to describe an individual identified by means of a cross-sectional survey of a neighborhood. By "activist" is meant someone who has a reputation for doing things in an area and whose efforts or expertise are valued even though that person does not necessarily hold any official position or role in an organization. *See also* INFORMAL LEADERSHIP, OPINION LEADER.

NONPROPORTIONAL CHANGE. A principle of biological growth in which the increase in size of an organism is accompanied by changes in its structure. More specifically the growth process requires that given relationships of the parts of the organism set limits to the change process. Insects are limited in size because they lack a bone structure. To double in size an object must more than double its skeletal structure. If a community increases its population by half, its organizational patterns may become twice as complex.

OPINION LEADER. The individual who acts as a clearinghouse and interpreter of information between the larger society and some local social group. Originally drawn from voting studies in the 1940s and 1950s in which people were often found to rely on key people in their immediate environment to accept or reject messages coming from the mass media. *See also* INFORMAL LEADERSHIP.

PARAPOLITICAL STRUCTURE. A term widely used in relation to theories of political change and community analysis. It refers to the variety of groups, affiliations, and loyalties which comprise a web of associations whose activities and composition serve as key elements in political processes although often without direct intent, specification, or conscious purpose.

PAROCHIAL NEIGHBORHOOD. An identified local area in which people feel a strong loyalty with each other, share many values in common, and have little contact beyond their local setting.

PLURALISTIC IGNORANCE. The social situation in which individuals presume that their own behavior is distinct from or similar to that of others in their social setting when in fact the opposite is true. Thus people in a given neighborhood assume everyone is apathetic and will not take action when in fact many people are or have been in contact with city agencies.

PLURALISTIC POWER STRUCTURE. A pattern of decision-making or influence in which clusters of individuals can be identified and function somewhat independently of one another in contrast with a "monolithic power structure" where the same persons appear to wield influence in a wide variety of situations. *See also* POWER STRUCTURE.

POWER STRUCTURE. A set of identifiable persons whose reputations, roles, or decisions form a network of common ties and contacts over an extended period of time with respect to a specific geographical or population domain.

REDUCTIONISM. The view in the behavioral sciences, particularly sociology and psychology, that all human behavior is explainable at the level of the individual personality. This view devalues the role of social structures and groups as explanatory constructs.

REFERENCE GROUP. A concept derived from sociology and social psychology which denotes identification by an individual with some social entity—past, present, or future. The behavior of the person therefore can be understood by knowing the norms which that entity defines for the behavior of its members. Social influence by means of reference group theory means that a state of mind exists which can negate the presumed "objective" group identities attributed to a given person.

RELATIVE DEPRIVATION. A theory of social change and individual attitude which implies that the standard for evaluating one's situation in the world is largely a function of how one stands with regard to another reference group. Poverty is not measured by real income or by comparing one's past earnings but by the position of those who seem to deserve the same fate. Thus blacks may be earning twice the income they did ten years ago but they observe that whites have gained two and a half times as much.

REPUTATIONAL ACTIVIST. *See* NEIGHBORHOOD ACTIVIST, POWER STRUCTURE, INFORMAL LEADERSHIP.

SELECTION, SELECTIVE RECRUITMENT. Social processes by which groups are able to determine who can and cannot become members of the group. In regard to neighborhoods, this may be a self-imposed process or one determined by the residents. In the case of an organization, qualifications and regulations can produce the same result.

SOCIAL CLASS. A broad term used to denote significant clusters of common characteristics shared by individuals in the same society and demarcating them from others. This usually implies a hierarchy of values—material, behavioral, and attitudinal—which distinguish those with more or less of the attribute used to rank individuals.

SOCIAL COMPRESSION. A term used to denote the limited physical and social mobility of individuals with reference to some standard of differentiation found in other populations. With reference to the black ghetto it means the restricted residential movement and consequent increase in social diversity which results from a growing population with constrained spatial and institutional alternatives.

SOCIAL DIFFERENTIATION. The process by which individuals distinguish themselves from others either in objective material ways or in subjective cultural and attitudinal ways. In its more complete sense it refers to the creation of social classes.

SOCIAL-EMOTIONAL LEADERSHIP. *See* EXPRESSIVE LEADERSHIP.

SOCIAL FUNCTION. *See* FUNCTION.

SOCIAL INTEGRATION. The level of effective interlock between different social patterns and institutions found for a given population or community. Often this is assumed to be increased by homogeneity but is likely to be the result of how closely meshed are such institutions as families, neighborhoods, associations, and formal agencies of government. While perfect integration is not possible it is also not desirable. But a range of points along a continuum can be identified and the effects of each compared.

SOCIAL STRATIFICATION. The creation within a given population of distinct levels of honor, deference, material rewards, or valued behaviors usually conceived of in terms of some hierarchical ordering from highest to lowest.

SOCIALIZATION. The process by which individuals are influenced by those with whom they interact. As a person spends more time in a given setting it is likely that he, other things being equal, will more come to reflect the attitudes, behaviors, and values of those who have been in that environment longer. This contrasts with a process of selective recruitment where the person is likely to resemble his peers even when he is brought into the group. *See also* SELECTION.

STATUS. A term of widely debated precise meaning in the behavioral sciences but most frequently used in our discussion to refer to a position as measured by socioeconomic level.

STATUS CONFLICT, CONFRONTATION. A characterization of a group, organization, or neighborhood in which perceived differences in status are recognized and extensive.

STATUS HETEROGENEITY. A condition of extensive variation in the composition of a group, neighborhood, or organization with regard to demographic attributes such as income, education, occupation, age, or sex.

STATUS INCONSISTENCY. A term used to denote a situation where the individual has multiple status criteria which do not correspond. Terms such as "status crystallization" and "status congruence" refer to the fit between the individual's status and that which is typical of his peers. Thus status inconsistency can be used to refer either to differences among ranks using the norms of a whole population or to the relationship between a given indicator (such as income) and what is typical of those living in the same neighborhood.

STRUCTURAL, STRUCTURE, SOCIAL STRUCTURE. Considering neighborhoods, groups, and organizations as institutionalized patterns of problem-solving. In particular, a way to think about how individuals relate to one another apart from their motivations for doing so or their individual preferences.

STRUCTURAL ALIENATION. Those patterns of neighborhood, groups, or organizations which tend to reduce the probability that a given population can effectively contribute to the overall goals of those parts of a community so as to advance the goals of that community.

STRUCTURAL ISOLATION. The extent to which the institutions of a given population are not linked up with the resources and power necessary to meet the goals of its individual constituents.

SYSTEM ALIENATION. The set of individual attitudes which see the solution to problems as a function of collective action to change the way in which existing institutions of the community function, but where such action cannot be advanced within existing political or parapolitical forms.

VOLUNTARY ASSOCIATIONS. Organizations covering a wide variety of purposes characterized by broad-based or local membership in which participation is not obligatory. While church and labor unions are traditionally included in such groups they tend to be more involuntary in practice. *See also* LEADERSHIP DISPLACEMENT, PARAPOLITICAL STRUCTURE.